Adult Language Learners: Context and Innovation

Edited by Ann F. V. Smith and Gregory Strong

Maria Dantas-Whitney, Sarah Rilling, and Lilia Savova, Series Editors

TESOL Classroom Practice Series

 TESOL Teachers of English to Speakers of Other Languages, Inc.

Typeset in ITC Galliard and Vag Rounded
by Capitol Communication Systems, Inc., Crofton, Maryland USA
Printed by United Graphics, Inc., Mattoon, Illinois USA
Indexed by Pueblo Indexing and Publishing Services, Pueblo, Colorado USA

Teachers of English to Speakers of Other Languages, Inc.
1925 Ballenger Avenue, Suite 550
Alexandria, Virginia 22314 USA
Tel 703-836-0774 • Fax 703-836-6447 • E-mail tesol@tesol.org •
http://www.tesol.org/

Publishing Manager: Carol Edwards
Copy Editor: Sarah J. Duffy
Additional Reader: Terrey Hatcher
Cover Design: Capitol Communication Systems, Inc.

ISBN 9781931185615
Library of Congress Control No. 2009930531

Table of Contents

Contents

Acknowledgments

We would like to thank our respective families, Eric and Annamay, and Kathi, for their ongoing support throughout the evenings and weekends devoted to this project. In addition, we appreciate the assistance and encouragement offered by our series editors and from colleagues Elizabeth Gatbonton and Barbara Sinclair, who reviewed the introduction and provided suggestions. Finally, sharing and developing ideas with our contributors and with each other has made the coediting process both a rewarding and developmental experience.

Ann F. V. Smith and Gregory Strong
Volume editors

Series Editors' Preface

The TESOL Classroom Practice Series showcases state-of-the-art curricula, materials, tasks, and activities reflecting emerging trends in language education and in the roles of teachers, learners, and the English language itself. The series seeks to build localized theories of language learning and teaching based on students' and teachers' unique experiences in and out of the classroom.

This series captures the dynamics of 21st-century ESOL classrooms. It reflects major shifts in authority from teacher-centered practices to collaborative learner- and learning-centered environments. The series acknowledges the growing numbers of English speakers globally, celebrates locally relevant curricula and materials, and emphasizes the importance of multilingual and multicultural competencies—a primary goal in teaching English as an international language. Furthermore, the series takes into account contemporary technological developments that provide new opportunities for information exchange and social and transactional communications.

Each volume in the series focuses on a particular communicative skill, learning environment, or instructional goal. Chapters within each volume represent practices in English for general, academic, vocational, and specific purposes. Readers will find examples of carefully researched and tested practices designed for different student populations (from young learners to adults, from beginning to advanced) in diverse settings (from pre-K–12 to college and postgraduate, from local to global, from formal to informal). A variety of methodological choices are also represented, including individual and collaborative tasks and curricular as well as extracurricular projects. Most important, these volumes invite readers into the conversation that considers and so constructs ESOL classroom practices as complex entities. We are indebted to the authors, their colleagues, and their students for being a part of this conversation.

Adult language learners are goal oriented and direct their learning to fulfill particular needs or demands: to advance their studies, to progress up the career ladder, to follow business opportunities, to pass a driving test, to assist their children with homework, or simply to be successful users of the language. They usually require immediate value and relevance from their studies, and they often learn best when they are engaged in developing their own learning objectives.

In examining learning environments as varied as Brazil, China, Iran, Japan, Thailand, the United Kingdom, the United States, and Vietnam, *Adult Language Learners: Context and Innovation* deals with three main areas of education. The first section focuses on language teachers as adult learners themselves developing their teaching practice. The second focuses on different means of expanding learner autonomy, an important trait of the adult language learner. The third deals with innovative classroom practices. By reading these chapters you will gain an overview of recent developments in adult language learning and of ideas and techniques that can be easily adapted to your own teaching context.

Maria Dantas-Whitney, Western Oregon University
Sarah Rilling, Kent State University
Lilia Savova, Indiana University of Pennsylvania

CHAPTER 1

Adult Language Learners: An Overview

Ann F. V. Smith and Gregory Strong

Today, World Englishes and English as an international language (EIL) are of increasing importance in international communication, business, the media, and pop culture. They have also gained importance in research journals and in such fields as civil aviation. Broad estimates of the number of people studying English are extremely large, and this number is growing, particularly among young adults. Graddol (2006) suggests that current trends may result in a spike of some two billion English language learners in the next 10 to 15 years, and he envisions a time when English language ability may well become a baseline skill in countries where English is taught as a foreign language today.

Accordingly, English language education has assumed greater importance in adult education. In this book, we focus on adult language learners in the hope of providing inspiration and ideas to English as a foreign language (EFL) and English as a second language (ESL) teachers, teachers in training, and volunteers. We use the term *adult language learner* to distinguish these learners from younger language learners enrolled in primary and secondary schools; these groups possess very different characteristics from adult language learners.

Adult language learners are goal oriented and direct their learning to fulfill particular needs or demands: to advance their studies, to progress up the career ladder, to follow business opportunities, to pass a driving test, to assist their children with homework, or simply to be successful users of the language. They usually require immediate value and relevance from their studies, and they often learn best when they are engaged in developing their own learning objectives.

These attributes, distinct from those of younger language learners, led to the creation of the term *androgogy,* a word popularized in the 1980s to distinguish the field of adult learning from that of pedagogy. Adults are mature, competent, experienced, multitalented individuals who live complex lives and fulfill a variety of different life roles. They can draw on this wealth of previous life and educational experience for their learning, but they may learn in very different ways. Some prefer a more process-oriented approach with active experimental

1

problem-solving tasks over memorization, whereas others may prefer learning styles developed during their school years (Knowles, Holton, & Swanson, 1998). This early view of adult language learners as unique, complex individuals coincides with constructivist theory (Williams & Burden, 1997).

As language learners, adults have multifaceted identities in their dynamic and changing lives. They can usually communicate confidently and effectively in their first language (L1) and may code switch between several other languages. They may be immigrants or international students, professionals, workers, or refugees. They may have their own interpretations of their culture and belief systems as well as the ability to reflect and build on their cross-cultural experiences. Some are highly literate in their L1, and others are illiterate. Some may struggle, as many of us do, to move from beginners to capable users of the additional language. Most also want to develop their own identities as users of the language and realize that it is unrealistic to measure their progress against a native speaker model. V. Cook (2002) recognizes language learners as having multiple competencies because their languages create different interconnections in their minds compared to monolingual speakers. He suggests that "learning an L2 [second language] is not just the adding of rooms to your house by building an extension at the back: it is the rebuilding of all the internal walls" (2001, p. 408).

Research has also shown that adult learners have greater cognitive and linguistic capabilities and conceptual complexity than younger learners (Robinson, 2005), although these capabilities (e.g., attention span, information processing of a rich and complex range of input, memory storage capacity) may vary from learner to learner. In addition, adults are able to discuss their learning styles and strategies in ways that children and adolescents are unable to (Cohen, 1998). In recent years a more positive view of adult language learners has developed, despite intense debate and sometimes conflicting research into the central claim of the *critical period hypothesis* that adult learners cannot gain full mastery of an L2, especially native-like pronunciation (Griffiths, 2008).

The humanist approaches from the 1970s also offer insights. Considering the whole person as an entity, with sensitivity to feelings and emotions, fits well with the concept of the adult language learner that can be found in the literature. The importance of developing confidence and self-esteem is paramount (Williams & Burden, 1997), and a relaxed learning environment reduces anxiety, which in turn improves motivation and confidence.

Research into the importance of learner identities, learner competencies in second language acquisition (SLA), and their relationship with learner autonomy has recently been revisited. Autonomous adult language learners show many of the characteristics previously noted in studies of good language learners and lifelong adult learners. Terms and phrases such as *active, able to manage, critically reflective, self-confident, self-determining, motivated,* and *responsible for learning* are frequently found. Benson (2007) indicates that "language learners are more capable of autonomous action . . . than teachers typically suppose" (p. 24) and can determine both content and learning strategies. However, learners develop various ways to achieve their different degrees of autonomy, and some may need to embark on a scaffolded process to gradually develop greater autonomy.

Since publication of Skehan's (1989) influential work, adult language learner traits, learning styles, and strategies have been reconsidered alongside developments in cognitive and educational psychology, aptitude, motivation, and SLA. Learning styles and learning strategies are problematic concepts because there are many different typologies that overlap with each other and with personality. Personality factors, such as introversion and extroversion, continue to influence learning because extroverts tend to be more fluent in complex verbal tasks. However, adult language learners can employ strategies to monitor and evaluate their own learning during a particular task. Cohen (1998) points out that learners apply strategies in different ways depending on their individual preferences, their personalities, the task, and a number of other factors.

Language aptitude is now considered to be a combination of several cognitive factors, including working memory, phonological coding and decoding, and L1 learning and literacy skills. Motivation also focuses more on a multifaceted learner who is dedicated not only to today's struggles but also to sustained effort over a period of time. Dörnyei (2006) suggests that learners' goals include a concept of an *ideal L2 self* and a more extrinsic *ought-to L2 self* and the learners move between "the actual self and his/her ideal or ought-to L2 selves" (p. 54).

Certainly, any discussion of adult language learners must mention the influence of the immediate learning situation and the future context. Norton and Toohey (2001) suggest that adult language learners have multiple identities, wide-ranging potential, and a vision of future options, including the possibility of belonging to and participating in an imagined future community context. The dynamics of the learning context both inside and outside the classroom have significant influence. Learners who become involved in local social contexts gain opportunities to interact using language in real and relevant situations.

Both in the community and in the classroom, adult language learners need an accepting, secure, and supportive environment that engages them. So the teacher must foster in students a willingness to cooperate and collaborate with each other. By listening actively, eliciting and asking questions, and sharing opinions, students learn together and develop into a cohesive group. Although Vygotsky's (1978) focus on social constructivism and the dynamic interaction between the learners, teacher, task, and learning context concentrates on young learners, its spotlight on the importance of a secure social context is also relevant for adult learners (Williams & Burden, 1997).

Therefore teachers should access or develop materials that meet the specific needs of the adult language learners in their particular contexts, whether EFL or ESL, workplace or academic. Developing these materials can involve the teacher and the learners in negotiating aspects of the syllabus and setting goals via self-evaluation processes and individualized learning plans. In addition, Jenkins

(2006) advises teachers to consider EIL and whether native-like pronunciation is appropriate in their context. She suggests helping learners find out "about Englishes, their similarities and differences, issues involved in intelligibility, their strong links between language and identity and so on" (p. 173).

Learner-centeredness increased significantly with the advent of the communicative approach to language teaching, although many variations now exist. The focus of communicative language teaching (CLT) on using meaningful language in context involves being able to use language appropriately in situated transactional and interactional environments as well as knowing the rules. Hedge (2000) notes that CLT develops five interlinked competences: discourse, strategic, linguistic, fluency, and the highly contextualized pragmatic competence. She suggests that most adult language learners can already utilize these skills in their L1.

In recent years, the popularity of task-based instruction has led to the investigation of task construction and linguistic complexity. Real-life tasks provide comprehensive input and frequently involve adult language learners interacting in group projects. Task types can be manipulated to develop fluency, complexity, appropriacy, accuracy, and confidence. Integrating tasks with a focus on form means that grammatical competence, once a major focus of language instruction, has regained its value within linguistic competency (R. Ellis, 2005b).

Increasingly, technology also is embedded into language tasks and syllabus design. Adult language learners have opportunities to upgrade their skills via webquests (Dodge, 2007) and podcasts, and to create blogs and broadcasts in order to contribute to and feel part of the community around them. In addition, spoken and written corpora increasingly provide opportunities for adults to expand their lexis through collocations, prefabricated lexical phrases, and fixed phrases rather than from simply using bilingual word lists. In the adult classroom, innovative teaching can integrate stimulating and enjoyable tasks into a congenial classroom environment to provide occasions for engagement, collaboration, investigation, and critical analysis of content, context, culture, and structures.

USING *ADULT LANGUAGE LEARNERS: CONTEXT AND INNOVATION*

In examining learning environments as varied as Brazil, China, Iran, Japan, Thailand, the United Kingdom, the United States, and Vietnam, *Adult Language Learners: Context and Innovation* deals with three main areas of education. The first section of the book focuses on language teachers as adult learners themselves developing their teaching practice. The second focuses on different means of expanding learner autonomy, an important trait of the adult language learner. The third deals with innovative classroom practices.

The chapters in the book have been selected so as to provide the reader with an overview of important aspects of the field, with emphasis placed on classroom practice rather than theory. Much of our work as editors of this volume has been to strike that balance between theory and practice.

TEACHER DEVELOPMENT

The first part of this volume looks at teacher development from several perspectives. Brandt (chapter 2) begins by investigating English language teacher certification programs around the world. Drawing on her research, she describes how these programs often overlook the importance of local contexts, and she suggests a number of ways to address this problem. Next, because all teachers need to keep up with developments in SLA that influence classroom practice, McCormack (chapter 3) presents an overview as well as classroom tasks to aid the teaching of SLA to new teachers.

Kim (chapter 4) relates how future teachers can learn both content and new technology when embedded into a teacher education course. In this case, the teachers collaborate to create a permanent resource that they can share. Baker, Crawford, and Jones (chapter 5) also provide a creative approach to teacher education through the use of e-portfolios. They remind us that teachers as well as students need to see themselves as lifelong learners. Ding (chapter 6) discusses the topic of teacher enthusiasm, encouraging teachers to actively engage adult language learners and to solicit their help in assessing teacher enthusiasm so that teachers can maintain and enhance it. To close this section of the book, Duong (chapter 7) describes why memorization is used so extensively in EFL teaching, sometimes inappropriately, and how there might be a larger role for memorization in ESL contexts.

EXTENDING LEARNER AUTONOMY

This second section of *Adult Language Learners* shows how a variety of approaches to curriculum design can promote greater learner autonomy. In a key discussion, Murray (chapter 8) conveys the quintessential features of a self-directed university language course for Japanese learners, and his approach can be employed by teachers interested in developing similar courses to enhance learner autonomy. Moving to a U.S. community college ESL literacy course, Lamping (chapter 9) details how to use a participatory approach to foster mutual support among a group of learners. Then Alexander (chapter 10) demonstrates how teamwork among adult learners working in a graduate research module can be developed when teachers negotiate with students and help them learn how to work together.

In his contribution, Andrade (chapter 11) transforms the familiar book report assignment into an interactive group activity. His structured process and question templates have the extra benefit of making plagiarism, now so common a problem (with book reports and summaries available on the Internet), much more difficult. Next, Dias (chapter 12) shows how the expanding educational potential of the Web can be harnessed to help students develop critical thinking skills. In this case, the class project (creating online presences for nonprofit organizations) empowers learners to act on issues that concern them.

In the last chapter of this section, Ghahremani-Ghajar, Mirhosseini, and Fattahi (chapter 13), who are Iranian teachers in the highly specialized field of medical English, describe a distinctive language discovery approach. It offers students a means of acquiring language through transferrable personal, community, and Web-based research into the medical conditions of family members and friends.

INNOVATIONS WITHIN A COURSE

The third and final section of the book looks at innovations that can be incorporated into a given course. Strong (chapter 14) describes an ethnographic approach to learning about language and culture through field trips in an EFL environment. In developing oral skills, Stillwell (chapter 15) explains how role-plays coupled with controversial topics can become an effective means of teaching discussion skills. Smith (chapter 16) also addresses discussion skills through a short case study based on a local yet globally relevant issue, which provides an effective means of teaching reading and discussion skills to adult language learners.

Through a radio drama project, Kubanyiova (chapter 17) demonstrates a highly motivating vehicle for adult language learners that can be done relatively simply using tape recorders. Finally, Augusto-Navarro, de Abreu-e-Lima, and de Oliveira (chapter 18) outline how course design, especially in an English for specific purposes setting, should incorporate ongoing needs analyses of the adult language learners, their expectations, and the context.

These chapters have been selected with classroom applications in mind. We hope that by reading them you will gain an overview of recent developments in adult language learning and of ideas and techniques that can be easily adapted to your teaching context.

Ann F. V. Smith is an English for academic purposes (EAP) tutor at the Centre for English Language Education at the University of Nottingham, in England. She has extensive experience as a TESOL/EAP teacher, teacher educator, examiner, and materials developer in Asia, Scandinavia, Canada, and the United Kingdom. Her publications focus on syllabus design, case-based teaching, and classroom practice.

Gregory Strong is an English professor and program coordinator at Aoyama Gakuin University, in Tokyo, Japan. He has also worked in China and Canada as a teacher educator and curriculum designer. He has contributed to various TESOL books and has published fiction and the biography Flying Colours: The Toni Onley Story *(Harbour Press, 2002).*

Teacher
Development

CHAPTER 2

Thinking Locally, Training Globally: Language Teacher Certification Reappraised

Caroline Brandt

English language teaching (ELT) is now a thriving international industry, so every year many people consider career options in ELT, or teaching English to speakers of other languages (TESOL), as it is sometimes known. The field attracts school and university graduates with little or no work experience as well as those with several years of experience in the workplace, which may or may not be education related. There are several routes into the profession, and anyone wishing to train as an ESOL teacher is likely to face decisions that will be influenced by a variety of factors, including his or her qualifications, previous experience, availability of time and funds, and the country in which he or she is based or wishes to train.

An increasingly popular and internationally available option, particularly for high school or university graduates as well as those who already have a teaching qualification or teaching experience in another field, is to take a short, intensive ESOL teacher preparation course, such as the U.K.-based Cambridge ESOL Certificate in English Language Teaching to Adults (CELTA). Such certificates offer a number of advantages, and several are internationally recognized, which can greatly improve an individual's employability and mobility. Programs tend to be comparatively short (around 120 hours, excluding independent study) and so may be conveniently completed during a vacation, for example. They do not require any prior teaching experience, nor are applicants required to hold a college degree. Although some applicants (graduates, for example) may be eligible to apply for a place in a diploma or master's degree program, the investment in terms of time and funds required to take a certificate is significantly less. This makes it attractive to prospective ESOL teachers who may use a program to gauge their commitment to the field before embracing the demands of graduate study.

An additional feature of the programs discussed here is that they are all aimed at teaching participants how to teach adult learners. This situation readily leads to terminological confusion because it involves two sets of students (student teachers and language learners) as well as three distinct groups of people who teach (trainers, participants, and experienced teachers). In an effort to avoid confusion, therefore, throughout this chapter I refer to those running the kind of ESOL teacher preparation programs discussed here as *trainers*; those who are learning to teach ESOL by participating in these programs or courses as *participants*; those who are learning English as *language learners*; and the experienced teachers whose teaching the participants are required to observe as *ESOL teachers* or simply *teachers*. In all cases, however, the people concerned are adults. Comparable programs for preparing ESOL teachers to teach young learners are also widely available but are excluded from this discussion.

Such programs, partly to ensure their international recognition, tend to have a centralized structure; that is, their structure, syllabus, length, design, and applicant criteria are standardized and regulated, and the program is run locally with relatively minor adaptations made to account for the local context. This chapter discusses the impact of this centrally planned and locally implemented (CPLI) approach on participant experience. It is suggested that trainers in particular need to become aware of the impact so that they can take account of it in how they run their programs. For example, a CPLI approach tends to lead to the broad representation of learning as a question of the transfer of knowledge from trainer to participants, which has been found to be in contrast with not only the needs of program participants as adult learners but also the "ideology of TESOL" (Richards, 2001, p. 213) that trainers conveyed in relation to teaching language learners. To provide a specific example, the CPLI approach appears to respond poorly to adult learners' need for a more transformative approach that encourages them to articulate their reflections and metacognition. Trainers who are aware of such matters can take steps to counteract their effects.

The chapter concludes by suggesting several program features that could be readily implemented in the short term to improve both the training process and the participant experience. These features include the provision of resources in independent learning centers for participants and activities aimed at the development and expression of new teachers' skills.

CONTEXT

The CELTA is one example of the kind of short, intensive ESOL teacher preparation programs that take a CPLI approach and that are the focus of this chapter. Other examples include the Trinity College London Certificate in TESOL (CertTESOL), the U.S.-based SIT Graduate Institute TESOL Certificate, and several less well-known programs that take a comparable approach. Such programs account for the induction into the profession of well over 14,000 people per year. CELTA programs alone currently account for the training of more than 10,000 people per year through some 900 programs held in 286 centers in 54 countries (*Certificate in English Language Teaching*, n.d.), and CertTESOL programs are taken by more than 4,000 people per year through approximately 120 institutions in the United Kingdom and other countries (J. Pugsley, personal communication, May 3, 2005).

The commercial success of CELTA and CertTESOL has influenced other providers, leading to a proliferation of comparable programs on an international scale. However, participants attending comparable programs are not reflected in the figures related earlier because such data are not widely available, owing in part to the scale and rapidity of their proliferation. The precise number of people who take such courses annually, therefore, likely far exceeds the 14,000 indicated by the available data.

Nevertheless, a significant number of programs have adopted a similar approach to training as that represented by CELTA and CertTESOL, in terms of their structure, syllabus, program length and design, and applicant criteria. They may also achieve a level of national or international recognition. One such example is SIT Graduate Institute's nationally (and, increasingly, internationally) recognized TESOL certificate (World Learning, 2009).

Although there are some differences between comparable programs and CELTA or CertTESOL, these tend to have more to do with the prominence assigned to components rather than to their presence or absence. For convenience, all such programs are referred to in this chapter under the umbrella term *CELTA model*.

Many programs are available that cannot be described as following a CELTA model. In these cases, significant features of the model may be absent or depleted. Examples include programs that are delivered online, which affects content and makes, for example, supervised teaching practice difficult, if not impossible. Such programs are excluded from this discussion.

CURRICULUM, TASKS, MATERIALS

Curricula

The CPLI approach is a defining feature of the CELTA model, and it has a number of implications affecting the curriculum, its implementation, and, therefore, the participant experience. For example, the syllabus criteria and guidelines are prepared in one location and distributed nationally and internationally. Local trainers then plan their programs according to the specifications provided, allocating time to components in order to ensure that the criteria are met. However, guidelines generally allow local trainers a little flexibility in terms of delivery. One of the main ways that such flexibility may be realized is in the decision to run programs as full time (one month) or part time (from approximately 12 weeks to 1 year). Another feature of the CPLI approach is that programs are monitored by a third party who ensures that central standards are met. This feature offers particular advantages in relation to a perceived need for standardization because employers of graduates of the same certification process expect parity between qualifications attained in different locations.

Programs are therefore available in different modes in many international locations. For example, CELTA programs are currently offered in locations that include Australia, the United Arab Emirates, and Vietnam, and CertTESOL program locations include Argentina, Hong Kong, and New Zealand. SIT TESOL certificates may be completed in Mauritania, Kyrgyzstan, or Costa Rica, among many other locations. Such locations represent significant diversity for participants in terms of several key parameters: the motivations and educational and language backgrounds of language learners; the impact of local culture, economy, traditions, and religions in the classroom; the status and role of English and ESOL teachers in the community; and the availability and type of opportunities upon graduation.

Programs following a CELTA model encompass the development of teaching skills and language awareness. Assessment is continuous, and there are no formal examinations. Curricula broadly consist of four components, though these may be arranged and labeled differently by different providers. Table 1 provides an overview of the various components of the three programs that are the focus of this chapter.

Supervised teaching practice and guided observation are key components of these certificate programs. The observation is referred to as *guided* because participants are required to complete a task while observing experienced teachers in the classroom. The aim of such tasks is to focus attention on relevant aspects of a lesson that, when possible, relate to a particular stage of the program.

In teaching practice, on the other hand, participants are required to teach for a minimum of 6 hours, and this component must be organized to allow them to teach two proficiency levels. All 6 hours of teaching practice are assessed. Guidance in terms of lesson plans and aims is reduced as programs progress. Participants are usually arranged into groups for this purpose and are required to collaborate in both planning lessons and observing each other's teaching practice. For the purpose of teaching practice, language learners are often drawn from the institution's enrolled population, attracted by the offer of free lessons. Feedback on teaching performance usually follows immediately after the lesson and tends to be carried out in groups, with all members being expected to contribute.

Recent research examined participants' experiences of such certificate programs. Data were gathered in two phases: a case study that involved 18 participants and 5 trainers attending a part-time program, and questionnaires received from 72 internationally located trainers and former and current participants. Outcomes included 26 issues considered critical in the preparation of ESOL

Table 1. Comparison of the Three Certificate Programs

Program	Components		Hours
CELTA	Input, tutorials, supervised lesson planning, feedback on teaching, peer observation, consultation		Approximately 100 hours
	Teaching practice		6 assessed hours
	Guided observation of experienced teachers		6 hours minimum
	Independent study consisting of reading, research, pre- and postsession tasks, assignments, and lesson preparation		80 hours minimum
Trinity College London CertTESOL	Five units: teaching skills, language awareness, learner profile, materials assignment, unknown language	Input (language awareness and methodology)	130 hours to include teaching practice (6 hours minimum), guided observation (4 hours minimum), learning unknown language (4 hours minimum) plus unspecified number of hours of independent study
		Teaching practice	
		Guided observation of experienced teachers	
		Journals (x 3), written assignments, interview with a Trinity moderator	
SIT Graduate Institute TESOL Certificate	Workshops, lesson planning, and analysis		130 hours to include teaching practice (6 hours minimum) and observation (4 hours minimum)
	Practice teaching and feedback		
	Observation		
	Written assignments and independent study		Unspecified

Source: *CELTA Syllabus*, n.d.; Trinity College London, 2006; World Learning, 2009.

teachers (for the complete list, with discussion, see Brandt, 2007). It was found that most participants and trainers considered their particular certificate program to be highly successful in achieving the aim of producing effective ESOL teachers. However, those involved in the research raised a number of issues connected with the quality of the training experience.

Teaching Practice

Teaching practice in CELTA, CertTESOL, and the SIT TESOL certificates was usually organized to provide each participant with two consecutive trainers over the duration of the program. Most participants welcomed this, believing that it would improve their chances of success because if the relationship with one was unsatisfactory, there was an opportunity for this to be redressed with the other. However, some participants felt obliged to familiarize themselves with both of their trainers' particular preferences so that they could teach accordingly and be rewarded for doing so. Some participants believed that the path to success lay primarily in identifying different trainers' preferences and expectations and then performing accordingly.

In terms of the techniques that participants were expected to acquire and demonstrate, several felt that these ran counter to their own preferences or instincts. Consequently, some experienced anxiety when asked to do something they did not agree with, see the relevance of, feel confident performing, or understand. Many participants also described finding that they were expected to prioritize the demonstration of these techniques in teaching practice and that this was sometimes at the expense of focusing on learners' needs in lessons. This led to references to language learners as "a means to an end" and as "guinea pigs solely . . . to practice on." Some trainers were aware of this situation, agreeing that they tended to prioritize participants' performance. This prioritization might further have been at the expense of the language learners because it emphasized the demonstration of technique over response to the learners' immediate and incidental needs.

In relation to their language learners, participants also found that learners attending teaching practice differed in various ways from those attending regular classes. For example, they observed that learners could be "primed" through having prior experience of teaching practice classes. It was found that trainers frequently recycled plans and materials given to participants, particularly in the early stages of teaching practice. Consequently, participants sometimes found that their teaching practice learners were prepared for the experience of being a language learner in a teaching practice class, to the extent of knowing material and expected responses by heart. Trainers were also aware that "real" language learners could differ from teaching practice language learners, observing that the latter group could be more cooperative and more forgiving than the former.

Feedback After Teaching Practice

In feedback, all participants were usually expected to comment on their peers' lessons. However, participants understandably preferred to avoid the confrontation that tended to result from giving negative feedback and on occasion were observed to enter into "pacts" with their peers, whereby one party would agree not to offer negative feedback to the other in return for reciprocal behavior from the other party. Participants also became increasingly focused on their own survival and performance as the program progressed. Such factors led them to take progressively less interest in each other's performance and, in some cases, to resent the time spent engaged in attending their peers' feedback sessions.

Participants considered a good relationship with the trainer to be essential for success in teaching practice, likely to lead to more positive feedback after teaching practice and to a better overall result. Consequently, their anxiety was increased when the relationship was poor because participants believed that they could fail the course as a result. It was also important to participants to have the opportunity to justify what they had tried to achieve in their teaching practice class. However, they quickly discovered that there was little available time for this, and they described their frustration about this situation and their belief that it arose as result of the momentum of the program, which could not easily be broken.

Lack of time also prevented participants from seeking clarification or more information at times. For example, as might be expected, trainers differed in their interpretation and application of the objectives and criteria. Several participants complained that there was little time or opportunity to ask for clarification in this matter and said that they were "just expected to accept everything without any explanation or discussion." Others noted that their trainers held differing views; for example, one participant observed that "what one would find acceptable and worthy of compliments, another might condemn. And there was no explanation or discussion of this."

Participants also found that their peers could make comments that were inconsistent with those of their trainer. This situation was often prolonged because trainers did not have sufficient opportunities to address the inconsistency. Participants also described receiving feedback that was inconsistent with their own views but were reluctant to question it because of time pressure. For example, one participant noted that "sometimes our . . . group would be asked to give our comments and then the [trainer] would say something completely different. Then we would go away confused."

Observing Experienced Teachers

Some trainers recognized that there were differences between what they teach participants to do and what participants observe the experienced teachers doing. They felt that this could be acceptable if they had the opportunity to discuss reasons for this with participants; however, the opportunity to do so was precluded, largely due to lack of time. Participants likewise found that they were sometimes required to demonstrate skills that they rarely saw being demonstrated by experienced teachers. Experienced teachers, however, were aware of this and on occasion took deliberate steps to display the technique or skill that they knew participants expected to see, even when the activities did not fit in well with their plans.

Collaborating With Peers

Participants described the experience of collaborating on a teaching practice lesson as very useful in the early stages because they enjoyed working together and learned from each other. However, this aspect became increasingly problematic as the program progressed. In the later stages, participants reported anxiety because collaboration created opportunities for peers to use others' ideas. This was felt to be threatening in the competitive context of assessment, in which many participants were desperate to receive and retain credit for their own ideas. For example, one participant observed, "Teaching practice planning—we are [having] problems with [participant 1]—there's a difference between an 'exchange of ideas' and 'pinching ideas.'"

In addition, some participants felt that the time required for effective collaboration was not justified by the benefits. They experienced unfairness in terms of the quality or quantity of time and effort each member of the group put into tasks, and they found that they did not have time to address such problems. For example, one participant noted that "the necessity for group collaboration resulted in too much support time and too little effective work time. Collaboration was very expensive in terms of time relative to learning." Others felt that in their programs the focus was more on individual survival rather than on any benefit to be gained from teamwork, as this participant observed: "There is a need to survive that can make people selfish. Sometimes the stronger participants get to the stage where they won't help the weaker ones because they fear they will fall behind."

Participants' Learning

Several trainers commented that their program was particularly suited to a certain type of participant. A trainer in Portugal summed up one as the kind of person who

> learns very quickly, is willing to accept that learning by making mistakes is an acceptable way to learn, is not defensive, is a good team player, is able to switch off from the grades and concentrate on the process, can work under real pressure, can apply theory to practice effortlessly.

This trainer felt that those who do not fit this model are at a significant disadvantage, particularly those who require more time to develop the necessary skills.

REFLECTIONS

The practice of short, intensive ESOL teacher preparation programs as described in this chapter raises a number of issues related to the CPLI approach and to the local design issues of program intensity, content delivery, design features (such as the way teaching practice is organized), and flexibility of response to participants' needs as these change in the course of their development into teachers. In particular, the CPLI approach significantly affects the model of learning represented to participants. Learning broadly appears to be expressed as a question of transfer from trainer to participant, perhaps paralleling the transfer of syllabus from central organization to local center. Learning as transfer, in the conditions described here, has a number of features. It is expert directed (trainer has it, participant needs it) and may be subordinating (central organization takes precedence over local center, trainer over experienced teacher, trainer and teacher over participant, participant over language learner). It is replicating (participants are expected to copy recommended techniques, with few opportunities to reflect, question, or experiment with alternatives). It is inflexible (not responding well to individual participants' preferences or to their development over time; nor can it easily take account of local conditions and contexts). And finally, it is dependent (participants are dependent on trainers for feedback and believe that their success or failure is linked to the quality of their relationship with their trainer).

This model of learning stands in sharp contrast to current understandings of adult learning processes, which suggest that successful adult learners are able to appreciate their own learning processes and benefit from discussion and reflection on them. They build and reflect on experience, encounter considerable learning that is incidental and idiosyncratic, learn through reflective learning that is unique to each person, and are able to reorganize experience and see situations in new ways. Adult learning is therefore potentially transformative, personally and socially (Tusting & Barton, 2003). There is also evidence to suggest that adult learners learn more deeply and effectively if they are actively involved in designing their own learning experiences (Light, 2001).

In recent years, attention has increasingly been paid to understanding successful adult learning in relation to the adult language learning classroom (e.g., Richards, 2001). It is ironic that less attention seems to have been paid to the conditions and contexts in which adults learn how to teach ESOL, despite the fact that these adults are ideally placed to learn about learning from a number of perspectives and to convey these understandings through the instruction they provide to their own language learners.

Addressing and reconciling such issues is clearly a long-term project, given the variety of international contexts in which these short, intensive ESOL teacher preparation programs take place and their scale. In the short to medium term, however, there are a number of steps, more immediately and readily implemented, that could significantly improve the experience for many participants. These steps would also enable trainers to incorporate greater integrity into their programs by meeting several of the conditions required for optimal adult learning. Because program validation cannot be achieved without meeting the criteria and standards specified in central documentation, these steps take the form of additional program features:

- *Shift the emphasis from training to development.* Start by viewing the development of professional competence in TESOL less as a question of replicating technical expertise, or training, and more as education or development underpinned by collaboration, reflection, and dialogue, with learning as its pivot.

- *Prepare participants for all aspects of the experience of attending a certificate program.* Encourage participants to prepare to take a certificate program, not only in terms of its content but also in terms of learning how to learn.

This may be particularly necessary in the case of those whose last experience of formal education may have been some time prior to training (see Brandt, 2006).

- *Develop participants' skills of critical thinking, reflection, metacognition, and teamwork.* Workshops could be aimed at developing participants' skills in these areas and their understanding of learning processes (their own and those of language learners). These workshops could be provided early on.

- *Add white space to the schedule.* "White space" added to participants' schedules could allow time for reflection and absorption of information.

- *Assign participants to a mentor.* Participants could be assigned to experienced teachers in a mentor capacity, allowing the participant to shadow the teacher, encouraging collaboration rather than observation alone. Participants would observe routine lessons rather than contrived ones.

- *Encourage participants to identify, utilize, and build on the skills and attributes that they bring with them to the program.* Activities could be included to help participants identify the skills that they already possess, which could make them more effective teachers.

- *Provide unassessed teaching practice opportunities.* Additional opportunities to teach practice classes could be made available to participants. This would give them the opportunity to teach and practice free from assessment pressure.

- *Avoid using recycled plans and materials.* Instead, guide participants to make genuine efforts to identify and address their language learners' needs and to prepare fresh lessons based on those needs.

- *Encourage a view of certification as the first step in a process of lifelong professional development.* Activities that encourage participants to view certification as beginning a process of lifelong professional learning and development could be included throughout and continue after the program has ended.

- *Provide an equipped independent learning center for participants.* The equivalent of an independent learning center that is widely available for language learners could be made available for participants. In this way, the participants could develop areas of their teaching that were identified as weak by their trainers.

- *Heighten awareness of different teaching contexts.* A range of activities could be included that are aimed at heightening awareness of different teaching contexts. These could help draw attention to the realities of the work situation for qualified TESOL teachers in various situations worldwide (Ferguson & Donno, 2003).

This chapter raises a number of issues and questions in relation to the international initial certification of ESOL teachers. Many of these issues appear to result from the application of a centrally planned but locally implemented approach to teacher certification. This may be inevitable given the international scale of the operation, as there is a perceived need for standardization to ensure parity between qualifications provided by centers representing one scheme but operating in a wide range of different contexts. In particular, it seems that the CPLI approach leads to a situation in which the novice teacher experiences conflicting models of learning. He or she experiences a broad transfer model while learning to teach language learners according to more transformational principles.

We have, therefore, a situation in which our practice as teachers of language learners appears to be more closely aligned to best practice than is our practice as trainers of novice teachers. This in turn suggests that teacher preparation in ESOL lags behind language teaching, where it might reasonably be expected to be leading by example. However, we can begin to reconcile the two spheres of practice through the implementation of several additional program features. As these features are readily implemented within the constraints of most current certification contexts, it is hoped that trainers worldwide will reappraise their practice in the light of these recommendations, to improve a process that is without doubt, from many perspectives, highly successful.

Caroline Brandt teaches communication skills to undergraduates at the Petroleum Institute, in Abu Dhabi, in the United Arab Emirates. She is the author of Success on Your Certificate Course in English Language Teaching: A Guide to Becoming a Teacher in ELT/TESOL *(SAGE, 2006) and* Read, Research and Write: Academic Skills for ESL Students in Higher Education *(SAGE, 2009).*

CHAPTER 3

Mind the Gap:
Second Language Acquisition
Theory Into Practice

Bede McCormack

Courses in second language acquisition (SLA) theory and research have for many years been a staple of master's degree programs in teaching English to speakers of other languages (TESOL). Such courses, however, can sometimes fail to promote a meaningful connection between SLA theory and classroom practice. Time and again, student teachers' precourse assumptions about language learning get the better of them, and they develop lessons based on repetition, mimicry, and memorization. By not making a connection between SLA theory and classroom practice, they may fall back on the assumption that one teaching approach will suit all learners (the "It worked for me!" approach), that difficult concepts need to be explained and every error corrected.

This chapter describes how the gap between theory and practice in a master's course might be bridged by involving students in tasks such as presentations, online discussions, video recordings of student teacher practica, and lesson planning that reflects effective teaching methodology.

CONTEXT

The ethnic, cultural, and linguistic diversity of New York City creates a high demand for qualified English as a second language (ESL) teachers. New York does have state standards for adult ESL learning, but there is no certification process in place comparable to that for K–12 ESL teachers. This has meant that institutions involved in teaching adult ESL learners have increasingly taken it upon themselves to ensure that their teachers have a recognized level of teacher training. Community colleges, language schools, and classes run by community-based organizations now generally require evidence of training such as an ESL certificate or a full MA in TESOL or applied linguistics. New York City adult ESL teaching positions are no exception. If enrollment figures are anything to go by, an increasing number of those intending to teach ESL in the city are opting for the MA.

The MA TESOL in the School of Education at Hunter College reflects the diversity of New York City. Many of the students are immigrants themselves or are the children of immigrants. Many have attended New York City public schools (perhaps even as ESL students), are the first in their families to graduate from college, and are now preparing to return to the community as ESL teachers with an MA in the field. With their diverse backgrounds, they often draw on their own experiences to illustrate many of the issues raised during their SLA courses.

CURRICULUM, TASKS, MATERIALS

The SLA course at Hunter College is typically taken toward the middle or end of the MA program, after students have completed a prerequisite course called Structure of English as well as others on materials, methods, and curriculum design. Equally important, by the time students take SLA, they should have completed a significant number of hours (50–100) of fieldwork, during which they observed a variety of adult ESL lessons. The fieldwork not only helps them see the connections between theory and practice, but also provides students with contacts among classroom teachers to whom they can turn for data collection projects.

The SLA course begins by laying a foundation in the history of linguistics, general learning theory, and psychology. The intention is to contextualize SLA, to give it a place in history as a development and synthesis of other fields. In this way, students can draw on their background knowledge to fit the course content into their existing schema. Visualizing the main paradigms of second language acquisition and their related pedagogical approaches and classroom practices helps students grasp this (see Table 1).

Table 1 attempts to summarize the history of thinking on second and foreign language acquisition. The left column indicates the broad theories, the middle column focuses on the pedagogical approaches of those theories, and the right column identifies specific classroom practices associated with those approaches. The table presents more recent SLA theories at the top, along with their associated approaches and practices, and more distant and historical theories, approaches, and practices as one moves down the table. Although language socialization, along with Lantolf's (2000) and Ohta's (1995) associated socio-cultural approach, has appeared most recently in the field, the greatest amount of SLA research continues to be done within the framework of the interaction hypothesis.

This research in turn has led to a number of suggestions for classroom teaching, most notably Long and Crookes's (1992) task-based language instruction

Table 1. Second Language Acquisition: Theory to Classroom Practice

Theories	Pedagogical Approaches	Classroom Practices
Language socialization Focus on learner as complex social being (Watson-Gegeo, 2004)	Sociocultural approach (Lantolf, 2000; Ohta, 1995)	• Cooperative learning activities that provide opportunities for language, cognition, and culture acquisition through learner–learner interaction
Interaction hypothesis (a) Focus on learner–learner negotiation of meaning to arrive at set outcomes (Long, 1996) (b) Overt form instruction and feedback to students are contextualized (Doughty & Williams, 1998)	Task-based language instruction (Long & Crookes, 1992) Focus on form (Doughty & Williams, 1998) Noticing hypothesis (Schmidt, 1990) Corrective feedback (Lyster, 1998)	• Learners given increased autonomy to use authentic material to engage in multifaceted, ongoing tasks • Teacher as facilitator with discrete, intentional grammar instruction • Getting learners to notice input so that it becomes intake for acquisition • Limited and principled grammar (form) instruction and corrective feedback related to content in meaningful ways in order to maximize uptake
Meaning-based (a) Focus on learning and developing communicative competence (Hymes, 1972) (b) Second language (L2) seen as a system (interlanguage; Selinker, 1972), grammar taught inductively (c) Errors as indicators of systematic rule formation (Corder, 1967)	Natural approach (Krashen, 1982) Communicative language teaching (Widdowson, 1978) Functional/notional approach (Wilkins, 1976)	• Teacher-facilitated learning of systems of meaning over form • Increased learner role in lessons • L2 errors considered in terms of target language and first language (L1) • Instruction organized around contexts and purposes of language use
Behaviorism/structuralism (a) Focus on instructional practice (b) Errors to be avoided (c) L2 acquisition seen as habit formation	Audiolingual method (Fries & Fries, 1961) Contrastive analysis (Lado, 1957)	• Teacher-led intensive oral instruction • Teacher-led pattern drills, memorization • L2 and L1 compared, errors due to L1 "habits" • Degree of L1–L2 difference determines difficulty

(TBLI), an approach that has gained wide currency. In TBLI, learners use authentic material (i.e., material intended for native speakers, such as print periodicals and screen-based media) to engage in ongoing projects that require learners to use the target language to complete a variety of tasks with specified outcomes. Planning a trip, for example, might include going online to check schedules and hotel availability, calling for reservations, consulting maps and tourist literature, and so on. Despite the focus on meaning and interaction, interaction hypothesis–based teaching regards principled error correction as an important part of adult ESL classroom instruction, as described by Doughty and Williams's (1998) focus-on-form approach to error correction.

This approach eschews preselected forms for presentation and practice, and instead encourages teachers to identify learner errors as they occur during meaning-based instruction and address them at natural breaks in the task, within the context of that task. By drawing learners' attention to and having them notice errors in this way, focus on form attempts to both maintain the focus on communication and provide specific language instruction. This can be seen as a middle ground between older corrective-driven approaches to language teaching, such as the audiolingual method, and approaches that reacted against this, such as Krashen's (1982) natural approach in which there is little or no error correction at all. Selinker's (1972) interlanguage (IL) theory argues that, despite non-target-like aspects of a learner's second language production, it is nonetheless systematic and rule driven.

Using a graphic organizer like Table 1 to review various SLA theories gives students useful pegs on which to hang their own ideas. It helps them recognize how translation, repetition, and memorization in older approaches such as contrastive analysis and the audiolingual method can fit into more communicative styles of instruction. They also learn that some degree of narrow focus on form can at least create a setting conducive to acquisition, especially among adult language learners who expect to be taught in such a teacher-centered manner (Doughty & Williams, 1998; Long, 1996).

Additionally, recounting how these theories have changed over time gives students a sense of the ebb and flow of intellectual thought. By going beyond the course textbooks and including recent or controversial views, primary source documents can provide the detail and more up-to-date research that textbooks miss. For example, articles such as N. Ellis and Larsen-Freeman's (2006) discussion of the divide in the field between individual/cognitive approaches and social/contextual approaches provides a sense that the understanding of the SLA process is far from complete. Also, work such as that of Watson-Gegeo (2004) may appeal to students' sense of social justice. These kinds of readings suggest that a field such as SLA is constantly evolving and that students should realize that challenging accepted theory is healthy.

Minding the Gap Through Student Tasks

The issue of minding the gap between SLA theory and its classroom applications has been debated since Corder's (1967) call for teachers and researchers to recognize the importance of learner errors. As the corpus of SLA research grows, there is increasing confidence in stating implications for classroom practice. Activities that can help connect SLA research to classroom practice for MA students include student presentations, empirical data collection projects, online peer collaboration, video analysis of teaching, and lesson planning.

Student Presentations

One effective means of helping students make this connection is to have them create in-class group presentations on a selected topic that includes some related task for the class to do. By reading about a topic and preparing a 40- to 60-minute presentation, students become quite familiar with the content. The purpose of the task is to help the class see the connection between the theory presented and how it might be applied in the adult ESL classroom. Two potential topics are learnability theory and the aspect hypothesis.

Learnability theory proposes that certain aspects of language must be in place before subsequent aspects can be learned. This seems intuitive, but operationalizing it can be challenging. Two revealing areas of learnability theory are question formation and relative clause formation. In bridging the gap between learnability and the classroom, student presenters demonstrate how knowledge of this theory can help in identifying learner level. To do this, the presenters prepare data sets from a variety of levels of adult language learners that include evidence of question formation, relative clause formation, or both. This data can be from written work or transcriptions of oral recordings. Having done the assigned readings and heard the presentation, students look through the data in pairs, identifying examples of the target structures and ranking the learners' levels based on the complexity of their question or relative clause formation.

The aspect hypothesis proposes that first and second language learners alike first use perfective morphology (e.g., past tense *-ed* in English) in telic predicates (accomplishment verbs such as *read a book* and achievements such as *arrive*) and later extend this morphology to atelic predicates (activity verbs such as *run* and state verbs such as *love*). The hypothesis also claims that learners initially use progressive marking (e.g., *-ing* in English) on activity verbs and later with accomplishment and achievement verbs.

In making the connection between the aspect hypothesis and classroom practice, presenters can have their fellow students in the SLA course work with adult ESL learner data sets, written work, or transcriptions of oral recordings. Once the students have grasped the basic tenets of the hypothesis, they check the data for what morphology (past tense or progressive) the learners use with which verb type (telic or atelic) and rank them for overall complexity of use of the tense and aspect system. Understanding how verb type and morphology interact in this way can provide language teachers with another valuable tool for distinguishing learner proficiency levels.

A simple, student-led matching game is another way to effectively demonstrate the aspect hypothesis, and could even be used with higher level ESL learners. The objective is to first categorize verbs by lexical aspect (stative, activity, accomplishment, achievement) and then add appropriate past tense and progressive aspect morphology. This activity can be done by hanging newsprint for each lexical category on the classroom walls and then having students tape verb and morphology cards to the newsprint. An activity like this forces students or learners to think deeply about the connection between verb type and morphology.

Empirical Data Collection Projects

Another project that can help bridge the gap between theory and practice is one that formalizes the observation and action research students have done as part of their classroom practica by requiring them to design and operationalize a research question. Alone or in pairs, students identify and write a literature review on a topic; design questionnaires, tests, or other instruments to elicit data; submit formal requests to the college for permission to collect data from human subjects; and then conduct the experiments with their own learners.

One example of a project that lends itself nicely to survey data addresses Schumann's (1986) acculturation model of language acquisition, which holds that learner perceptions of and attitudes toward the target language community play a large role in determining ultimate second language attainment. This is realized in many areas, including the following:

- motivation

- gender

- age at first exposure to the target language

- degree of integration into the target language community

- role of identity and socialization as reflected in target language level

In working on this topic, students create surveys that attempt to elicit responses from their adult learners that roughly indicate the degree to which the learners feel motivated to learn and use the language, how integrated they are in the local community, how they feel, or the degree to which they perceive themselves as identifying with or rejecting the target language community. Questions are posed in terms of scenarios such as "If you were lost, how willing would you be to use English to ask for directions?" followed by a 5-point scale: "very willing, somewhat willing, somewhat unwilling, not willing, very unwilling." Results can be matched against overall learner level as determined by their score on a reported language test such as the Test of English as a Foreign Language or

International English Language Testing System, their age at first exposure to the target language, and their length of stay in the target language community.

The data treatments for these projects vary in complexity, with those who have had a course in language assessment conducting more ambitious projects and others looking more qualitatively at their data. Regardless of the approach, the project requires students to look in detail at aspects of language behavior in their own classrooms, consider what the literature says about the observed behavior, and arrive at some explanation for it. This project thus adds to the students' range of investigative tools with which to consider classroom language phenomena, furthering their ability to make principled curricular decisions based on SLA theory.

Online Peer Collaboration

Use of technology should be an integral part of an SLA course, and the course described here has a comprehensive online presence through Blackboard (see Blackboard, 1997–2009), an online suite of teaching resources. One Blackboard feature, online small-group discussions of instructor-set topics, allows students to share ideas, learn from each other, and provides less vocal students with a venue for their voices to be heard. Because many students taking the course are teaching or student teaching, the discussion board is an ideal place for them to report anecdotally on learner behavior that they notice in class. This is facilitated by the course instructor creating topics, such as the following, to focus students' attention:

- learner response to error correction (Do they notice they are being corrected? Does the correction lead to a change in their language behavior over the long term?)

- learner use of specific structures (e.g., pronouns, adverbs, articles, adjectives, modals)

- learner use of discourse features (e.g., speech acts)

- learner range of politeness registers

- pronunciation issues (e.g., ability to pronounce initial consonant clusters: *sch*ool, *str*eet)

- transfer of first language behavior into the second language (e.g., word order, phonology, reflexive pronouns)

Video Analysis of Teaching Practica

Another powerful technology that can connect theory to practice is the use of digital video. Students record aspects of ESL learners' language use in their own or a peer's class that reflects an SLA-related issue such as clarification requests, patterns of negation use, and reaction to corrective feedback. The student can then show the video in class, mention a theory that has addressed the learner's language issue, and lead a brief discussion by describing the context within which the behavior was observed and eliciting possible explanations for it from peers.

Lesson Planning

In an integrated MA program, the various courses must recognize each other's content and goals. In considering how lesson planning can be done within an SLA framework, students must look outside the SLA course to the program's ESL methods course. A fundamental part of any methods course is curriculum design and lesson planning, and one of the first considerations here is to consider adult ESL learners' needs, which can include several levels: content needs, sociocultural needs, and of course language needs.

Content needs may be determined by the ESL course type: academic, specific purposes, general communication skills, and so on. Sociocultural needs will be clear to students, the SLA course having introduced them to the notion of individual differences such as the role of age, motivation, aptitude, and degree of integration into the target language community. Surveys similar to those described earlier (see Empirical Data Collection Projects) can be used to obtain this information and inform curriculum design. Language needs can be generally recognized through placement tests that learners may have taken, but a more detailed understanding of their grammar, phonologic, and discourse needs may be gained through simple tests and other data elicitation instruments (e.g., recorded interviews, story retellings) used in SLA research. This detailed knowledge of the learners and their needs can allow teachers to adopt a differentiated teaching plan that accommodates learners' various backgrounds, personality, knowledge, and language skills.

Knowing their learners in some detail enables teachers to plan lessons, design activities, and select content based on learners' language and sociocultural needs. Lesson plans can include material designed to help learners notice targeted structures through some type of enhancement (e.g., bolding, underlining, repetition; Schmidt, 1990). Instances of error correction can be included in the plan in the form of short, contextualized focus-on-form activities as described earlier (Doughty & Williams, 1998). These activities address errors noticed by the teacher in previous classes and help him or her avoid spontaneous, on-the-spot error correction, which research has shown to have little effect (Lyster, 1998).

REFLECTIONS

As in the second language classroom, an SLA course should encourage students to take responsibility for their own learning. Despite misgivings that such practice might be misunderstood and perceived as avoidance of teaching responsibilities, students as well as colleagues are in near unanimous support of this more learner-centered approach. In conversations and on course evaluations, students comment that activities and projects like those discussed in this chapter enable them to interact with the content in meaningful ways. By making peer presentations, conducting classroom-based research, and collaborating online, students learn how to investigate, interpret, and report on language behavior that they observe in their classrooms. This in turn enables them to make informed, research-based pedagogic decisions and to prepare appropriate lessons that reflect developments in the field of SLA.

Bede McCormack holds a PhD from Durham University and has taught ESL/EFL in Japan, the United Kingdom, and the United States. He is currently the TESOL MA coordinator in the School of Education at Hunter College, City University of New York, in the United States. His research interests include teacher preparation and the impact of second language acquisition knowledge on teachers' pedagogical decisions.

CHAPTER 4

Podcasting and Online Journals as ESOL Resources

Deoksoon Kim

One of the challenges with technological innovations in educational practice is finding suitable ways to introduce them to new or preservice teachers as well as existing teachers hoping to upgrade their skills. Podcasting and online journaling are two such innovations. This chapter describes how these valuable resources can be used as tools to promote critical thinking and can be shared with other educators.

CONTEXT

In a teaching English to speakers of other languages (TESOL) course that I taught at the University of South Florida, podcasting and online journaling were part of a core assignment (Kim, 2009). The aim of the assignment was to create a case study portfolio of a language learner. The preservice teachers (whom I also refer to throughout the chapter as teacher trainees) each selected a language learner from kindergarten to the adult level, depending on the grade that they intended to teach. These language learners had varying levels of English proficiency, first language skills, and cultural orientations, and had lived in the United States for less than 3 years. According to Richards (1998), case studies "allow access not only to accounts of the problems teachers encounter but to the principles and thinking they bring to bear on their resolution" (p. xii), and they provide experience in a wide range of settings and contexts.

While enrolled in the TESOL course, the teacher trainees wrote online journals and created podcasts (online audio or video programs available for downloading to a computer or MP3 player) about their case studies while simultaneously creating a joint online ESOL resource center. Uploading the case studies to the ESOL resource center meant that they were available to help other teachers understand language learners' linguistic and cultural backgrounds and individual educational scenarios, giving those teachers the tools to solve learners' problems.

These resources engage teachers in a dialogue with real-life situations in specific school settings, which in turn provides scaffolding for their understanding of language learners in various social contexts.

CURRICULUM, TASKS, MATERIALS

This project consists of three main phases: (a) constructing language learner case studies, (b) journaling online for the written portion of the case study, and (c) creating podcasts and posting them to the ESOL resource center (Kim, 2009). The result is knowledge that is personally constructed and socially enriched: The preservice teachers create their own case studies and share them with others, thus enriching their learning and teaching experiences (Windschitl, 2000). In the same vein, Cole (1991) discusses the sociocultural constructivist theoretical framework. Four key elements of the sociocultural constructivist model of the teaching–learning paradigm in the English as a foreign language setting (learner, teacher, task, and context) interact with and influence each other to develop knowledge (Williams & Burden, 1997).

The online journals represented the detailed written case studies of the language learners (Kim, 2009). Online journaling combines text, images, Web pages, links to other blogs and podcasts, and other media related to the topic.

Podcasting may introduce new sharing and teaching strategies (Campbell, 2005; Kim, 2009; Richardson, 2006). This technology allows listeners or viewers to subscribe to digitally recorded files and send their own multimedia files to others via Really Simple Syndication (RSS). RSS is a Web-feed format used to publish frequently updated content such as blog entries and podcasts. By making new information readily accessible, RSS helps people keep up with their favorite Web content automatically (Richardson, 2006). Therefore, podcasting is a direct personal connection that caters to and embraces any audience size, and it offers transformative new information-delivery systems in educational settings, especially in higher education (Campbell, 2005).

The teacher trainees created the ESOL resource center by pooling their online journals and podcasts as a collection of valuable resources for teaching future language teachers about language learners, including adult language learners. These journals and podcasts were then placed in *Google Sites* (Google, 2009b) and *Ning* (2008; see Appendix for online resources), two Web sites that differ primarily in how open they are to the public. *Google Sites* is open to any Web user, so anyone can visit the ESOL resource center, which can be found at its uniform resource locator (URL), the global address of documents and other resources on the Web (in this case, http://sites.google.com/site/esol2spring2009/Home/). *Ning,* on the other hand, allows users to create social networks that are accessible by invitation only, so without a user name and password, visitors cannot access the ESOL network. If the project is to be shared among students in a class, *Ning* is the better choice. However, *Google Sites* offers more resources for collecting and managing case studies. The ELL case study portfolios were published with *Google Sites,* while the online discussions and blogs about and for the course were developed in *Ning* due to the sensitivity of the content.

To create the ESOL resource center, we used a variety of open-source programs and Web sites. Audacity and the LAME encoder (see Appendix) were used for this project because they are free and compatible for PC as well as Mac computers. For Web page construction, we used *Google Sites, Ning,* and *PodOmatic* (2009). Figure 1 shows the steps that the teacher trainees followed in completing the entire assignment.

Case Study

Through class discussions, the teacher trainees in the course identified the main points of each case study and developed their familiarity with the case study folio, which includes the written portions of the case study, audio files such as an interview sample, reading samples, writing samples, and other documents.

With the permission of the language learners they were studying, the teacher trainees (a) collected data such as observations, reading and freewriting samples, and interviews (including with the language learner's classroom teacher, as necessary); (b) analyzed multiple data sets; (c) created a problem scenario specific to the language learner; and (d) solved the problem, creating reflective discussion questions based on the case study experience. By taking these steps, the teacher trainees improved their understanding of the complexities of language learners' learning and literacy acquisition process.

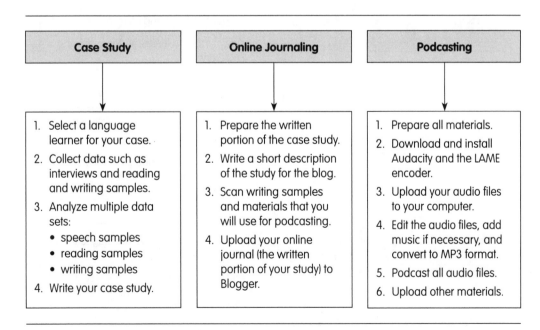

Figure 1. Steps of the Language Learner Case Study Portfolio Assignment

Online Journaling

The written portion of the case studies became the teacher trainees' online journals, which they uploaded to the Web using a blog tool. These journals included a description of the language learner, analysis of multiple data sets, a scenario of issues the language learner encountered, solutions and suggestions, and discussion questions to create a reflective teaching curriculum. The teacher trainees inserted links to their blogs on the ESOL resource center when they uploaded their podcasts and other materials.

Podcasting

Teacher trainees who were new to podcasting learned about it through such sites as Tech Ease (on *USF on iTunes U* [University of South Florida, 2007]), which offer accessible and explicit information about engaging in the process on PC as well as Mac computers. The Tech Ease tutorial podcasts demonstrate in detail how to podcast. As outlined in Figure 2, there are three major steps to the podcasting procedure: preparation, uploading audio files, and uploading online journals and other material.

Preparation

During this stage, the teacher trainees installed programs, created the script for a description of the case study, chose the layout of the screen, and prepared all

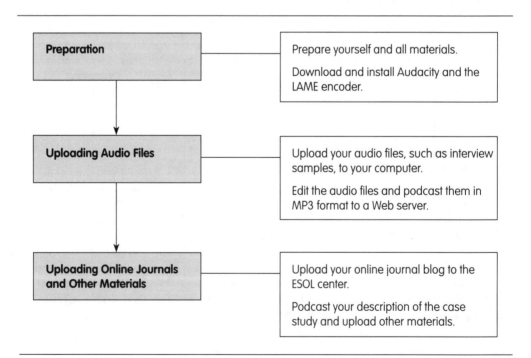

Figure 2. Podcasting Procedure

the materials for the case study (e.g., the written portion of the case study as a word-processed document, edited audio files, a scanned writing sample). They downloaded and installed the Audacity program and the LAME encoder (a free download for Windows and Mac operating systems). If they had Garageband on their Mac, they used that also to record their podcast.

Uploading Audio Files

Digital audio files were prepared using computers and other equipment such as MP3 players or digital recorders. As a learning experience, the teacher trainees recorded audio files of short interviews with each other, uploaded them to the computer, and edited them. Afterward, the teacher trainees interviewed their language learners and collected reading samples. They also recorded themselves briefly explaining their project. They prepared quality audio files by reviewing them, editing to remove noise, and adjusting the volume level. They also learned other tools to enhance their podcasts, including fade effects and how to add background music. Although the teacher trainees could add music during the editing procedure, for this assignment they were not required to do so. However, I made sure to remind them about copyright laws governing the use of sound recordings.

After editing, the audio files were converted from WAVE to MP3 file format to decrease the size, making them easier to distribute on the Web. Once the recordings were complete, the teacher trainees prepared an RSS feed and uploaded their podcast in MP3 format to a Web server. Alternatively, to keep things simple, they could use *PodOmatic*'s online service, which lets users record a podcast with their Web browser and a Flash interface (see, e.g., *Deoksoon's podcast,* n.d.). After testing their feed to ensure that everything worked, they posted the address for their podcast to the ESOL resource center in *Google Sites* so that they could subscribe to each other's podcasts. They were now podcasters!

Uploading Online Journals and Other Materials

The teacher trainees created their online journals using a range of blogging programs. They could also upload their word-processed case studies directly to the ESOL resource center. Once they had created their online journals or copied and pasted them from Microsoft Word into *Google Sites,* they entered the URLs of their podcasts into the journal. They then added graphics, PDF files, and pictures to their case studies using the main toolbars on *Google Sites.* Later, to invite an audience, the teacher trainees submitted their podcasts to a directory.

There are challenges to helping language teachers gain the skills to most effectively use new instructional media. However, some of the teacher trainees already knew about podcasting and online journaling, so they assisted others who were new to these applications. Implementing this new instructional technology step by step with hands-on demonstrations and suitable technical support did a great deal to reduce the anxiety that some teacher trainees felt, and eventually they were able to enjoy their success. One teacher trainee said, "It was rewarding for me, and I am glad to have a concrete project to show people." Another added, "My ESOL student and I enjoyed podcasting. He had fun listening to his voice. After listening to it, he tried to correct his English. It really motivated him to check his pronunciation and practice it."

REFLECTIONS

The power of instructional technology such as podcasting and online journaling introduced the teacher trainees' projects to a wide audience through the ESOL resource center. Other teacher trainees and teachers can access these projects and hear real language learners' voices in the podcasts. Having authentic voices reading samples and interviews is quite powerful and useful because it enables visitors to the ESOL resource center to reflect on issues faced by real language learners and learn from various case studies.

This project can be used for both teacher training and students' language development. However, instructors should be aware of a number of important issues. Copyright of sound recordings and musical compositions must be strictly observed, as must learners' privacy. We used pseudonyms to protect their identities, but sharing their works still can be sensitive. Thus, instructors should review and upload this material thoughtfully and obtain the appropriate consent forms from adult language learners, or from parents if the students are underage. In addition, instructors should recommend suitable Web sites for trainees to access and perhaps recommend that trainees use a more private network such as *Ning*.

Podcasting provides opportunities not only to track various students' language learning progress, but also to evaluate their language proficiency. And it can be used to teach the actual language. Using podcasting, the teacher may also upload students' oral presentations and then send the URLs of students' published work to parents, involving the parents more fully in the class.

Podcasting can easily be extended to teaching and learning at all levels. Sprankle's (n.d.) *Room 208* podcasts are a good example of how elementary school students can create their own podcasts. *Radio WilloWeb* (n.d.) also presents podcasts for kids made by elementary school students about various subjects, including science, social studies, history, and writing.

Students of any subject, at any level, can create podcasts to enhance their learning and their engagement with the content. As teachers, our classroom podcasts can serve as an excellent delivery mechanism, especially if we teach online courses. We can create episodes for specific modules to explain readings, and assignments, making podcasts an invaluable tool in distance learning.

Deoksoon Kim is an assistant professor at the University of South Florida, in the United States. She teaches second language acquisition and literacy, focusing on TESOL, second language reading and literacy, and instructional technology in teacher education. She has taught and done professional development and research in Korea and Canada.

APPENDIX: WEB SITES AND SOFTWARE FOR PODCASTING

Tools and Web Sites for Creating Podcasts

- Audacity: http://audacity.sourceforge.net/
- LAME: http://lame.sourceforge.net/
- Garageband: http://www.apple.com/ilife/garageband/
- *PodOmatic*: http://www.podomatic.com/
- *Google Sites*: http://sites.google.com/
- *Ning*: http://www.ning.com/
- *Blogger*: http://www.blogger.com/
- *WordPress*: http://wordpress.org/

Podcasting Tutorials

- *USF on iTunes U* (University of South Florida): http://itunes.usf.edu/ (click College of Education, and then Tech-Ease: Classroom Tech Help)
- *Teaching and Learning With Podcasting* (University of Wisconsin–Madison): http://engage.doit.wisc.edu/podcasting/teaching/index.html
- There's Something in the Air: Podcasting in Education (Campbell, 2005): http://www.educause.edu/EDUCAUSE+Review/EDUCAUSE ReviewMagazineVolume40/TheresSomethingintheAirPodcast/158014

Podcatchers and Podcast Directories

- *Podcast Alley*: http://www.podcastalley.com/
- *Podcast Bunker*: http://podcastbunker.com/

Student Podcasting

- *Room 208*: http://www.bobsprankle.com/blog/

Language Learning

- *ESL Podcast*: http://www.eslpod.com

CHAPTER 5

E-portfolios for Lifelong Teacher Development

Geoff Baker, Emma Crawford, and Martha Jones

This chapter describes the rationale behind the use of an e-portfolio in a distance learning English for academic purposes (EAP) teacher preparation programme. It provides specific information on using e-portfolios to promote reflective practice and learner autonomy, alongside examples of how we used them to facilitate continuous skill development.

CONTEXT

Although teaching EAP is becoming increasingly globalised, there is a paucity of EAP-specific teacher qualifications. The Postgraduate Certificate in Teaching English for Academic Purposes (PGCTEAP) offered by the Centre for English Language Education at the University of Nottingham is one of only a few credit-bearing programmes in the United Kingdom that focuses wholly on EAP. The programme is offered to experienced teachers of English as a foreign language who want to become EAP specialists by either face-to-face or distance learning mode. It enables participants to acquire the knowledge and skills necessary to help international students develop their academic language and study skills in order to meet the demands of undergraduate and postgraduate study in various university disciplines.

The e-portfolio was developed when the Centre for English Language Education recently introduced the distance learning version of this EAP specialist development programme, which attracted participants from all over the world, including China and the United Arab Emirates, as well as those from within the United Kingdom. The distance learning programme begins with a 2-week face-to-face introductory module, after which students return home and complete the other distance modules over the course of 8 months. The project outlined in this chapter evolved from the recognition, in light of engagement with pedagogical literature, of two key elements of successful distance learning: learner support and learner autonomy (Peters, 1998).

Learner support, the process of enabling students to take the most from their learning experience, is essential in ensuring that distance learners do not feel isolated. Thorpe (2002) maintains that successful learner support should be accessible and responsive to the demands of individual learners, highlighting the importance of interpersonal interaction. This does not necessarily need to be provided directly by the module teacher because members of an e-learning community can help each other learn by sharing ideas, constructing meaning together, and discussing important issues, all of which points to an interrelatedness that is likely to lead to successful learning (Clark, 2001).

Learner autonomy is both a central component of distance learning and a key aspect of EAP because the complexities of learning another language mean that students cannot restrict their learning to the classroom (Harmer, 2001; Oxford, 2003). At its most basic level, learner autonomy involves learners taking control of their own learning. To some extent, all distance learners must develop this autonomy because they have control over such factors as when they study and what they study; this does not always mean that they are learning in a completely autonomous manner, though, because they are often given specific instructions to minimise confusion about tasks (L. Murphy, 2007).

In anticipation of the commencement of the distance learning option, the Centre for English Language Education approached the Centre for Integrative Learning at the University of Nottingham for advice in providing effective learner support, promoting learner autonomy, and raising students' skills awareness. After consultation with the centre, we agreed that the creative use of an e-portfolio could address these issues, and the Centre for Integrative Learning provided funding and pedagogical support to introduce an e-portfolio into the EAP teacher development programme.

At their most basic level, e-portfolios are electronic repositories of an individual's information, which can be stored or presented in any format varying from a CD-ROM to a Web-based presentation. They have emerged as a pedagogical tool for a number of reasons, including their capacity to promote students' reflection on their own learning, a process that Daudelin (1996) describes as "stepping back from an experience to ponder, carefully and persistently, its meaning to the self" (p. 39). E-portfolios can also be used as methods of assessment, vehicles to promote student–student and student–teacher discussion and feedback, and learner organisation tools (Sherman, 2006). They can support differing aims and can either take the form of a prebuilt portfolio package (such as the e-portfolio strand of WebCT [see Blackboard, 1997–2009]), which can be adapted to suit individual needs, or be built specifically to a programme's requirements.

An e-portfolio was chosen from other possible teaching tools to promote teacher development on the distance learning EAP programme due to its capacity to contribute to learner support, help foster learner autonomy, and raise students' awareness of their own skills.

- *Learner support:* Most Web-based e-portfolios include some form of communication facility to enable participating students to discuss their progress with their teachers. Furthermore, the ability to showcase either the whole portfolio or selections of work to fellow students and the teacher means that e-portfolios have the capacity to work as communication tools through the feedback they provide. Effective use of this aspect of an e-portfolio can help mitigate feelings of isolation that distance learners sometimes experience, fostering a sense of community.

- *Learner autonomy:* An e-portfolio is a valuable tool for helping distance learners take control of their own learning. The owner of an e-portfolio has control over who can see specific areas of it, giving them a place to keep private thoughts or refine ideas until they are happy for others to see them. They have the right to invite guests from outside the course (perhaps family or employers) to see areas of their portfolio on the Internet and give feedback. In addition, although e-portfolios often allow for a basic framework of skills to be outlined, students should have overall control of what they contain. Finally, many e-portfolios attempt to foster a sense of agency through providing the capacity for self-evaluation. The ability to open them to comments from others means that there is an emphasis on peer as well as teacher feedback.

- *Skills awareness:* E-portfolios can help students record their progress towards the competencies required of a successful EAP teacher. This record can include reflections on lesson preparation, execution, and feedback. In addition to aiding student awareness of their own skills, the compilation of an e-portfolio allows for easier completion of job applications and résumés because students can draw on reflections and evidence from their portfolios. Furthermore, the e-portfolio embodies the reflective practice demanded of self-managing professionals and demonstrates this ability to employers.

There are a number of prebuilt Web-based e-portfolios available that can be adjusted to suit individual needs. After investigation, the WebCT e-portfolio was chosen for this project based on three main factors. First, WebCT was already being used as a virtual learning environment to support courses in the Centre for English Language Education, so students and staff were familiar with the interface. Second, the WebCT e-portfolio allows for the easy transfer of material from the virtual learning environment to the e-portfolio. With minimal effort, students can send contributions to group discussions, responses to exercises, and other contributions to the e-portfolio, where they can be catalogued and reflected on. Finally, the WebCT e-portfolio template structure was particularly suitable for creating the EAP teacher development programme portfolio outline. Expectations, structure, and instructions are given in the portfolio template, and learners retain control over the look and feel of their own portfolios and can add extra elements if they wish, which is central in promoting learner autonomy.

CURRICULUM, TASKS, MATERIALS

The WebCT e-portfolio was integrated fully into the programme, and the participating students were required to complete a number of tasks that were reflected on in the e-portfolio. These tasks were closely related to key subjects that participants studied during the course, and included six e-portfolio topics (see Table 1).

In addition to these specific tasks, participants also had the option of entering their reflections on any aspect of their learning, which could be made available to the teacher and other course participants at the e-portfolio compiler's discretion. Because this was the first use of an e-portfolio, it was decided that these reflections, and the e-portfolio as a whole, would not be assessed, though the reflections formed the basis for a number of assessed tasks. This decision was made to ensure that participants felt they had complete ownership of their portfolios and could be as candid as they wished in their reflections.

REFLECTIONS

The teachers of the distance PGCTEAP programme found the e-portfolio a valuable addition to the course. It provided a useful vehicle to maintain contact with course participants. It also made peer assessment and support far easier in a distance mode of course delivery, where these had been anticipated as possible problems. Furthermore, encouraging reflection on different aspects of the course seemed to help participants draw connections between the theoretical and practical elements of their learning. One teacher commented that the e-portfolio was "an excellent resource to help students keep track of their learning and identify the skills they have acquired during the course."

Participants' reflections on the experience of collaborative planning and teaching showed that they had conducted in-depth analysis of EAP teaching approaches, attitudes towards collaborative work, and acquisition of skills. The reflections varied in length and depth, but all students performed the task satisfactorily. When their e-portfolio material on this subject was ready, they sent a message to the module teacher and their peers inviting them to view and comment on it. When invited to comment on the use of the e-portfolio, most students highlighted the positive aspects of student control of the portfolio and the ability to share it with others.

Distance programme designers considering similar projects should note that it is crucial to fully incorporate the e-portfolio into the programme. Pedagogical literature emphasises the importance of embedding technology in the curriculum

Table 1. E-portfolio Topics

Key Subject	Participant Activity	E-portfolio Task
English for academic purposes (EAP) student needs	Interview international students about the preuniversity entry EAP programme. Identify study skills and language training that they require for their degrees.	Write an EAP student profile. Reflect on it individually and with the peer group in the e-portfolio.
EAP teaching skills (see Appendix)	Plan and deliver a lesson collaboratively in an EAP class.	Reflect on the experience in the e-portfolio. Share reflections with peers on the WebCT discussion board. Write an individual action plan to improve teaching skills.
EAP student autonomy	Design and pilot tasks and materials that facilitate student autonomy in a small-group situation.	Report on your findings in the e-portfolio. Reflect on the experience of supporting autonomous learning. Write recommendations on how to foster autonomous learning in EAP.
Norms and conventions of the academic context	Investigate an academic department. Identify what language and study skills training is needed by international students in that department.	Reflect on your findings in the e-portfolio. Use reflections for a written task.
Academic discourse	Select two journal articles, one from arts and one from sciences. Analyze the language, and design EAP materials to raise awareness of linguistic choices of specific disciplines.	Post your analysis in the e-portfolio. Reflect on comments provided by peers.
Teacher autonomy	Design a plan for ongoing professional development.	Share your plan with the teacher and, if desired, with peers. Gather insights and ideas.

and altering teaching practice accordingly, as opposed to merely annexing it to existing practice (Laurillard, 2002). To accomplish this, it is vital to ensure that the programme designers involved are familiar with the technical aspects of the chosen e-portfolio before they design the courses and materials. In the PGC-TEAP project, a number of workshops were run by the Centre for Integrative Learning's e-portfolio developer, who continued to offer technical assistance when required. This ensured that designers could harness the full resources at their disposal and helped avoid problems arising over basic technical issues. This was equally true for course participants, all of whom acknowledged the importance of ensuring that comprehensive training sessions were given beforehand, highlighting the benefit of the session at the start of the course. This does, however, raise an important issue concerning distance learning courses. The programme began with a 2-week face-to-face introductory module, which allowed for the provision of a comprehensive training session on site. In cases where an entire course is delivered via distance means, designers would need to ensure that participants were well informed about using the e-portfolio interface, perhaps through guidebooks and electronic presentations.

The project outlined in this chapter used e-portfolios to foster a sense of community for distance students in disparate geographical locations, promote learner autonomy, encourage reflection to connect theoretical and practical learning, and help students identify EAP skills developed through self-evaluation and feedback. Extending this example, e-portfolios can be adapted to suit students on placements and courses that require self-evaluation of teaching practice. Furthermore, e-portfolios are a useful tool for ongoing teacher development because they provide a forum for continuous reflection.

———

Geoff Baker is senior academic advisor at the Centre for Integrative Learning at the University of Nottingham, in England. He has wide experience using technology to support teaching and learning in higher education and has provided pedagogical support for a number of projects involving e-portfolios.

Emma Crawford is a learning technologist at the Centre for Integrative Learning at the University of Nottingham, in England. She runs pilot projects and evaluates the use of e-portfolios in learning and development for students and staff.

Martha Jones is head of teacher training in English for academic purposes at the Centre for English Language Education at the University of Nottingham, in England. She directs and teaches in teacher development programmes. Her research interests include corpus-based analysis of spoken discourse and the development and use of multimedia for teaching and teacher training purposes.

APPENDIX: EAP TEACHING SKILLS TASK

As part of the assessment of the face-to-face introductory module, course participants were required to collaboratively plan and teach a Listening and Notetaking lesson. Prior to the lesson, they received information on the group of students they were going to teach so that they could pitch the lesson at the right level.

After the lesson, participants discussed different aspects of their experience, such as what had gone well, what could have gone better, and how the lesson could be improved. At the end of the 2-week introductory module, course participants returned home and compiled their e-portfolio data on EAP teaching skills, one of six e-portfolio topics, based on the experience of planning and teaching a lesson collaboratively.

Aims of the Task

- to promote reflective and evaluative teaching practice

- to promote collaborative work with other course members

- for participants to link EAP theory to classroom practice

- for each participant to design an individual action plan to improve teaching performance in the future

Procedure for Compiling E-portfolio Data on EAP Teaching Skills

1. Course participants reflect on the collaborative planning process, taking into account how they contributed to the following:
   - focus of the lesson
   - overall aims of the lesson and aims of each stage
   - timing allocated to each stage
   - anticipation of problems and possible solutions
   - best possible exploitation of strengths and skills of members of the team
   - any difficulties encountered during the planning stage

2. Participants reflect on the lesson taught collaboratively. Using notes made immediately after the lesson, based on peer and student feedback, the members of the team reflect on the following:
   - advantages of collaborative lesson planning
   - collaborative analysis of feedback (student feedback and peer feedback)
   - participants' own thoughts and reactions in relation to feedback given

3. Participants post their reflections on WebCT to be viewed by teachers and peers.

4. Participants engage in a discussion on WebCT to raise any issues that may have remained unclear after they taught the lesson. This discussion enables them to expand their notes, which they can use to write their postlesson reflective evaluation, which is assessed.

5. After the online discussion, participants use their notes, read the messages posted by their peers on WebCT, and design a short- to medium-term action plan to improve specific classroom management or teaching techniques. This is developed in the e-portfolio, and participants make it available to their teacher and, if they feel comfortable, to their peers.

CHAPTER 6

Teacher Enthusiasm in Action

Peng Ding

The qualities of a good teacher almost always include being knowledgeable, well organized, empathetic, engaging, resourceful, and enthusiastic. This chapter considers the significance of the final quality, teacher enthusiasm, and ways for instructors to identify and develop their own enthusiasm. Csikszentmihalyi (1997) observes that teachers who often make a difference in students' lives are the particularly enthusiastic ones, who value their subject and show great dedication and passion, thus indicating that there is nothing else they would rather be doing than teaching. This chapter briefly introduces several pertinent theories of teacher enthusiasm and discusses the features displayed by two enthusiastic teachers working with adult language learners. Finally, a feedback chart is included, which teachers may ask learners or colleagues to complete in order to provide them with ideas about how to identify and maximize their enthusiasm.

CONTEXT

The most influential studies of teacher enthusiasm in the past have followed two main perspectives. Csikszentmihalyi (1997) and other education researchers, including Ericksen (1984), follow a psychological approach. They argue that teachers who show enthusiasm have great interest in and passion for their subject. The second, the behavioural perspective, focuses on distilling enthusiasm into more specific and countable behaviours. Collins (1978) designed an 8-point checklist of features that reflect teacher enthusiasm: voice, eye contact, gestures, movements, facial expressions, word selection, acceptance of students' ideas and feelings, and overall energy. More recently, Ding (2008) identified a number of core components of teacher enthusiasm that are essential if teachers are to be perceived as enthusiastic by students. These include sound subject knowledge, intrinsic interest in the subject, caring for students' learning, passion for teaching, genuineness (congruence), and rapport/interaction with students. I combined these components to form the first three categories in an Enthusiasm Feedback Chart (see Figure 1). In addition, a number of other accompanying factors can help teachers project and transmit their enthusiasm to students, including a teacher's personality, attitude, self-confidence, and presentation skills. In terms of personal characteristics, enthusiastic teachers frequently show features such as a high level of expertise, humor, liveliness, and cooperation as well as dynamic body language and speech (which is reflected in the fourth category in the Enthusiasm

---

Lecturer's name: _____ Lecture topic: _____

Part 1: Categories
Please give your opinions about the enthusiasm of your teacher and how his or her teaching affects your learning. Fill in the chart anonymously. Underline any negative comments. The table shows some aspects of teacher enthusiasm to assist you.

Subject Knowledge and Skills	Intrinsic Interest and Passion	Interaction With Students	Animation, Speech, and Body Language
Knowledge: provides a comprehensive look at a subject and aspects of culture and society *Language:* offers vocabulary and grammatical structures *Teaching:* is willing to try new ideas and approaches	*Commitment:* shows a genuine interest in the subject *Presentation:* makes lessons interesting and easy to follow *Illustration:* uses real-life examples, and shares personal experiences	*Atmosphere:* creates a relaxed yet productive classroom *Rapport:* shows interest in students, chatting with them and learning their names *Culturally sensitive:* refers to and shows interest in students' culture(s)	*Voice:* varies inflection *Facial expression:* uses expressions to show emotion; eye contact reaches every student *Gestures:* uses hands and body to communicate

Your Opinions

Part 2: Scale
Please rate the following indicators of your teacher's enthusiasm on a scale of 1 (very low) to 6 (very high) by ticking (✓) your choice.

Distant	1____	2____	3____	4____	5____	6____	Friendly
Indifferent	1____	2____	3____	4____	5____	6____	Passionate
Lethargic	1____	2____	3____	4____	5____	6____	Energetic
Uninformed	1____	2____	3____	4____	5____	6____	Knowledgeable

Figure 1. Enthusiasm Feedback Chart

Feedback Chart). These qualities help the teacher motivate and inspire students (Ding, 2008).

During a professional development program at the University of Nottingham, in England, a group of secondary school English language teachers from China had the opportunity to discuss teacher enthusiasm. These Chinese teachers were well placed to provide insights into enthusiasm from both an adult learner's and a teacher's perspective and to make comparisons of enthusiasm in the United Kingdom and China. They identified four instructors, three European (one Scottish, one Hungarian, and one Slovakian, all teaching in the U.K. context) and one Chinese (teaching in the Chinese educational context), as particularly enthusiastic teachers. The Enthusiasm Feedback Chart (see Figure 1) was used to select these enthusiastic teachers.

CURRICULUM, TASKS, MATERIALS

Interestingly, the Chinese teachers found that each of the four enthusiastic teachers showed certain similarities. However, these instructors also demonstrated certain idiosyncratic behaviors as well, which echoes Salmon's (1988) observation that "where pupils catch fire, it is the teacher's fire they catch. And it is a *uniquely* personal fire" (p. 37). For example, the Hungarian teacher's top five enthusiasm attributes were an intrinsic interest in the subject, pleasant personality (e.g., outgoing, sociable, genuine), great care for student learning, dynamic body language and speech, and positive attitudes toward every aspect of teaching (e.g., lesson, learners, subject). Meanwhile, the Scottish teacher shared some attributes, such as an intrinsic interest in his subject and dynamic body language and speech, but he also differed in terms of other attributes: He displayed showmanship, he seemed more interested in his own performance and seemed to care less whether the students were learning, and his relationship with students seemed detached. These latter three aspects somewhat prevented the conveyance of his enthusiasm to the Chinese trainees.

Teachers should analyze the features that make their enthusiasm more prominent. For example, an introverted teacher and an extroverted teacher can both be enthusiastic, but they will show enthusiasm in different ways. However, teachers should be true to their personalities, so the introvert should not copy the animated gestures, sometimes extravagant body language, and dynamic speech of the extrovert. Teachers should transmit their enthusiasm through methods with which they are confident and comfortable. Effective teachers who are naturally introverted convey their enthusiasm by displaying their deep knowledge and affection for their subject. Good and Brophy (2000) argue that "teachers can use dramatics or forceful salesmanship if they are comfortable with these techniques, but if not, low-key but sincere statements of the value that they place on a topic or activity will be just as effective" (p. 238). If a teacher is enthusiastic, even in a more reserved way, an adult learner will quickly detect this.

As mentioned previously, teacher enthusiasm is idiosyncratic and varies from one class to another. Ding (2008) claims that teachers can effectively transmit their enthusiasm to students by doing the following:

- Display a genuine interest in student learning, and avoid detachment.

- Exhibit your passion about the course and your field of study.

- Have a thread of issues that you want to teach, but allow other thoughts and ideas to unfold (i.e., leave space for enthusiasm to grow).

- Risk new ideas and approaches in the classroom.

- Refrain from overdisciplining students.

- Show that you care about students and their learning progress.

- Use big, open gestures and dynamic speech.

Besides these general strategies, two cultural awareness strategies are also worth mentioning:

- Be positive about students' cultures.

- Empathize with students' culture shock.

Drawing on these strategies, the Enthusiasm Feedback Chart in Figure 1 can help teachers gather feedback from colleagues during teacher observation or from adult language learners. Teachers can hand out this form in class and ask participants to fill it out anonymously, noting when they feel the teacher's enthusiasm in class. Teachers can then identify which demonstrations of enthusiasm seem to have a positive impact on students' motivation and interest in learning. It might even be useful to videotape a class for a more complete analysis. In addition to asking students to complete the chart, teachers might also wish to use the chart with their peers as a discussion point when reviewing their teaching practice.

Once completed, the Enthusiasm Feedback Chart will suggest which components of enthusiasm the students feel are their teacher's strongest attributes. Teachers can then try out some of the suggested strategies for improving enthusiasm in their teaching and adopt them if they are effective. However, teachers must be careful not to view enthusiasm as being an equal balance of all components contained in the chart; content knowledge is clearly a key component.

REFLECTIONS

Teachers need to adjust their enthusiastic behaviors and methodology to suit the students' cultures. For example, they may present more grammar and use less body language if their students are Chinese. Instructors should also reflect on their pedagogical skills as well as their unique personal traits. By comparing their perception of their demonstration of enthusiasm with the feedback, they can further develop their potential and avoid any attributes and practices that may discourage student enthusiasm.

Adult language learners can detect genuineness in teaching, and they will pick up on a teacher's passion for a subject. As one of the Chinese observers proposed, "Don't be afraid to show that you are emotionally attached to the subject you are teaching!" As teachers, we need to show our passion for what we teach and, in so doing, kindle students' interest in learning.

———————————

Peng Ding has a PhD in applied linguistics from the School of English Studies at the University of Nottingham and an MA in English linguistics from Beijing Foreign Studies University, where she worked as a lecturer of English. Her interests include teacher and learner motivation and teacher enthusiasm in second language acquisition, teacher training, and cultural differences in second language education.

CHAPTER 7

Memorization in Language Teaching: Vietnam and the United States

Duong Thi Hoang Oanh

The role of memorization in language teaching is controversial, particularly among native- and nonnative-English-speaking teachers working in English as a foreign language (EFL) environments. In many EFL teaching environments, for reasons outlined in this chapter, memorization is employed extensively, sometimes at the expense of communicative language teaching. However, language teachers everywhere employ some memorization in their classrooms for teaching vocabulary, collocations, and certain key grammatical structures to their students.

This chapter compares two different educational contexts. In one, the language teaching was undertaken in an EFL classroom in Vietnam, a context in which memorization plays a central role. In the second, a communicative language teaching methodology was used with adult learners in an English as a second language (ESL) classroom in the United States. I compared these two classes using questionnaires and observations, which were followed by in-depth semistructured interviews with the two teachers and a total of four students (Oanh & Hien, 2006).

The comparison of these two classes has several goals. First, I hope it encourages ESL teachers to gain a better understanding of the previous language learning environments that their students may have experienced. Second, it may help prepare teachers who have studied or taught communicative language teaching and are now planning to teach EFL in an international context. Additionally, I hope that EFL teachers presently using memorization will better appreciate its limitations. Understanding the role of memorization in these two educational contexts may also assist language teachers in both to appreciate the contribution that its use may provide.

CONTEXT

The first class was a third-year public speaking course in a BA in English program for 45 Vietnamese students, ages 19 to 24, at a university in Vietnam. This once-a-week 45-minute class aimed to prepare students to deliver effective formal and informal speeches, and to prepare them for oral tests, job interviews, and future professional communication. It also helped students with other classes that required oral presentations as part of the classroom practice and assessment. The second class was an oral presentation course for English language learners at a university in the United States. For 10 weeks, the class met for 3 hours each week and focused on the oral presentation skills needed to be successful in a U.S. university. Ten students, in graduate as well as undergraduate programs, who were between 19 and 34 years old and came from a variety of countries, practiced oral communication and then made presentations, including lecturing on a given topic, fielding questions, and leading a discussion.

The role of memorization is often perceived as mindless rote learning in the United States, European countries, and other countries that use a communicative approach. But in many Asian contexts, repetition is seen as a route to understanding (Biggs, 1996). In Vietnam, it remains the chief language teaching methodology because there are few native-speaker models, little opportunity to listen to English-language media, limited access to authentic or updated materials, large classes of 50–60 students, and, in many places, poor teacher education. Moreover, overhead projectors and audiovisual equipment that would be taken for granted in many other countries are not always available. In addition, in Vietnam, as in many EFL contexts, memorization is used in several other content areas, for example, those that require learning of scientific formulas or that use memorized quotes or models to teach writing. In language classes, it is used to teach such aspects as new vocabulary, sentence patterns, and grammatical points.

Some ESL teachers characterize Asian students as being "raised in a conformist educational system . . . with memorising and reproducing information" (Harris, 1995, p. 78) so that they "rely more heavily on memorisation and less on understanding" (Samuelowicz, 1987, p. 123) and "place considerable emphasis on rote learning" (Harris, 1995, p. 78). Samuelowicz observes that for Asian students rote learning is common, leading to a noncritical reception of information and few initiatives being taken. In many cases, memorization is overused, such that all class activities involve memorization tests, leading to "bad memorization," which hinders the internalization of the language introduced in class.

However, numerous educators support some use of memorization as a teaching methodology. Mageean and Hai (1999) and Ramburuth (2001) describe memorization in Asian contexts and contrast the relationship between in-depth learning or memorizing (which involves understanding or "good memorization") with memorizing in a mechanical or rote manner. Memorization from understanding leads to reproductive capacity.

Other writers concur and discuss the link between deep memorization and activities for promoting automaticity, which in turns leads to fluency in speaking a language. According to Segalowitz (2000), teaching learners to employ a basic repertoire of commonly used phrases when communicating helps them create cognitive and performance fluency. In such a process, cognitive strategy and its two subgroups—learning strategies (rehearsal and elaboration) and using strategies (approximation and paraphrasing)—are most relevant to good memorization. These work directly and involve identifying, remembering, storing, and retrieving different linguistic aspects of the target language (O'Malley & Chamot, 1990).

Furthermore, Cohen and Oxford (2003) suggest that memorization has the power to increase attention, improve the encoding and integration of language material, and increase the speed of its retrieval for use. G. Cook (1994) contends that the repetition of parts of a language may help learners make better sense of vocabulary and native-like structures, which then become available for authentic and creative language use.

CURRICULUM, TASKS, MATERIALS

This section describes the tasks and teaching techniques in the two oral classes. In both, students first examined the principles of effective presentations. These included the selection of an appropriate amount of interesting and informative content as well as its logical organization and key points—focused, developed, and explained with good signposting for different parts of the talk. They also identified delivery in terms of a lively and enthusiastic manner, audibility, use of voice, pacing, appropriate nonverbal communication (including eye contact), avoidance of reading aloud, and adapting the talk to suit the audience. Students also examined language use, including correct use of vocabulary, grammar, and pronunciation. Students were also advised to choose suitable visual or audio support. Videos of effective and ineffective presentations and students' practice presentations were analyzed in class to enable students to identify and apply these features in subsequent presentations.

An outline of the classroom activities is provided in Table 1. In the class in Vietnam, the teacher introduced the principles and then followed up with group or pair presentations. In the U.S. class, principles were presented together with classroom practice.

Despite some similarities in content, there were obvious differences in the teaching practice in the two classes. In the large class in Vietnam, the teacher asked students to practice oral sentence patterns and mechanical drills, memorize vocabulary items, or choose famous speeches and identify and highlight words and phrases to learn by heart. For most of the speeches, the students were advised not to memorize the entire original speech, but only the most significant parts, such as the introduction and conclusion. However, for some short "model" speeches, students could choose to memorize the whole thing, and then they

Table 1. Classroom Activities

EFL Class in Vietnam	ESL Class in the United States
1. Examine the principles of good presentations.	1. Examine the principles of good presentations.
2. Find model oral presentations (e.g., famous speeches, narratives).	2. Choose words, phrases, or sections of speeches or good pieces of writing.
3. Identify the purpose of the speech (e.g., persuade, eulogize).	3. Review them for accurate pronunciation, comprehension, and tone of expression.
4. Use drills to memorize words, phrases, and sentence patterns from the speeches.	4. Recite them to other class members, expressing the exact emotion and message.
5. Perform parts of the speeches before the class while trying to convey the appropriate emotions.	
Additional Activities in Both Classes	
Approximation (using similar vocabulary, terms, and ideas), paraphrasing (using different ways to express the same meanings), dictation, vocabulary cards, a class vocabulary box, story reproduction (reading stories aloud, i.e., readers' theater), role-play, improvisations with extracts from famous plays, songs, poems, jazz chants	

performed these before the class, trying to capture the spirit of the speech in persuading their audience to a course of action or eulogizing something or someone. These activities provided students with the grammatical competence necessary for communication.

In the U.S. class, early in the course the students were given a list of famous short speeches and literary extracts to memorize. The teacher then called on students randomly to deliver these speeches. He started by throwing a small ball to each student as a signal for him or her to speak. Then that student passed the ball to another student to recite a speech, conveying not only the content but also the emotions behind it.

During each class, the teachers paid constant attention to each student during the process of reviewing and repeating words, phrases, and paragraphs of chosen stories or speeches in the performance of each activity. The teachers also focused on common mistakes that students made, their efforts to correct the mistakes, and their weaknesses and strengths in performing presentations. Students were advised to memorize meaningful units, along with the introduction and conclusion of their presentation, and to transmit "not only the content but also the emotion behind the content," as commented by the teacher in the U.S. class.

Common ground between the two classes argues for some use of memorization in teaching language. The benefits of memorization in certain tasks are explained in Table 2.

Both teachers concurred that memorization could be an effective strategy.

Table 2. Potential Benefits of Memorization

Set phrases of learning	Useful expressions that may not translate to other languages may have to be learned by heart for oral academic usage.
Vocabulary enrichment	Memorization can help students establish and expand their range and effective use of vocabulary and collocations.
Suprasegmental elements	Dialogues, speeches, songs, and poems can help students understand and efficiently use English intonation and rhythm in a native-like manner.
Social discourse	Certain social and cultural aspects of the target-language culture can be learned, enabling students to engage in social conversations comfortably and naturally.

They also agreed that good memorization, such as approximation and paraphrasing, might serve as a cognitive learning strategy undertaken to make learning easier, faster, more enjoyable, more self-directed, more effective, and more transferable to new situations.

REFLECTIONS

The teaching of these two classes shows some contrasts between how memorization is used. The Vietnamese teacher commented that "a foreign language is learned in a conscious and repetitive manner, to remember linguistic elements systematically to apply in use." She argued that although memorization alone cannot enhance communication, the acquisition of English in a non-English-speaking environment is difficult without it; memorized language input may be retrieved as soon as the need for communication emerges.

The U.S. teacher also recognized the usefulness of memorization, saying that although his students were immersed in an English-speaking environment, they still needed good memorization strategies, such as rehearsal and elaboration (making links between new information and previous knowledge), to create fluency and automaticity in learning English.

Classroom activities such as the ones described earlier helped promote memorization. One student said, "I am more prepared, with so many expressions and ideas that I could start and maintain my talk more fluently and respond automatically." Another added, "I am much more confident now using what I have learned. I know what I want to express. I am in control of my talk. My English is much more qualified and efficient, coming closer to a native-like level." But the U.S. teacher qualified the use of memorization, saying that poor memorizing doesn't help: "Students can only fluently utter memorized chunks at the beginning of a conversation, but lack the capacity and creativity for spontaneous and appropriate responses" (Oanh & Hien, 2006, p. 2).

Oral communication teachers may be able to usefully employ activities similar to the ones described in this chapter. Students in both classes stated that they enjoyed many of the classroom activities and remembered some linguistic details because of them. They felt that they had made gains in terms of accuracy and fluency.

In EFL and ESL contexts alike, memorization can be quite effective if used well. ESL teachers might consider utilizing it more than many do at present. However, if used mechanically or too frequently, as can occur in many EFL contexts, memorization may become an obstacle that hinders students' progress in becoming natural and competent communicators. Therefore, language teachers need to be vigilant, ensure its appropriate use, and recognize that it is but one of a variety of teaching techniques for oral communication.

Duong Thi Hoang Oanh is a lecturer and associate director of the International Cooperation Office at Hue University, in Vietnam. She teaches applied linguistics, curriculum design, and research methodology, and she researches educational reforms, intercultural communication, learner autonomy, and classroom practices. She has studied and researched in the United States, Canada, Australia, New Zealand, Singapore, and Thailand.

Extending
Learner Autonomy

CHAPTER 8

A Self-Directed Learning Course

Garold Murray

For the past 30 years, autonomy as an approach to learning and teaching has been gradually working its way from the margins to the mainstream in the field of language education. A focal point was the publication of Holec's (1981) report to the Council of Europe, in which he defined autonomy as "the ability to take charge of one's learning" (p. 3). For Holec, "to take charge" means that learners are responsible for all aspects of their learning, from goal setting to assessment. Since his report first appeared, a growing number of teachers have been faced with the challenge of how to create a learning environment that would enable adult language learners to undertake and fulfill these responsibilities.

One early response was to develop self-access centres where adult language learners could improve their proficiency through direct contact with target language materials. In these centres, learners are often shown how to learn a language through initial orientation sessions, workshops, advising sessions with experienced language teachers, and printed learning strategy or how-to guides. A current trend is to integrate self-access learning into language courses and programmes. In the few documented examples, self-access learning is made available as a module in a language course or as an elective course to compliment the main curriculum.

This chapter describes a required course in self-directed language learning developed for the English for Academic Purposes (EAP) Programme at Akita International University (AIU), in northern Japan. It begins by outlining the learning context, the rationale, and the principles that informed the design of the course. This is followed by a description of the course and an explanation of how it functions on a day-to-day basis. The chapter concludes with a reflection on the effectiveness of the course, some key issues, and the potential for its application in other language learning contexts.

CONTEXT

The self-directed learning course was developed for Japanese learners entering their first year of a 4-year undergraduate liberal arts programme. All first-year students at AIU must successfully complete the EAP programme before they can enrol in courses offered in either of the university's two programmes of study, Global Business or Global Studies. The medium of instruction in these courses is English. To fulfill their degree requirements, students must spend a year abroad studying at one of the university's sister institutions. Therefore, they are eager to learn as much English as they can in the shortest possible time.

The aim of the course is to help students develop English language skills as well as metacognitive knowledge and skills. Here, *metacognitive knowledge* refers to learners' understanding of how they can best learn a language, whereas *metacognitive skills* are those required to plan, monitor, and evaluate the learning (Wenden, 1998). To meet these aims, students are guided through the process of creating and carrying out their own learning plans. They are encouraged to experiment with a variety of materials, strategies, and activities, and to reflect on what works best for them as language learners.

Developing learners' autonomy is not one of the explicitly stated aims of the course; rather, autonomy is viewed as a key construct informing the design of the learning environment or structure (for a full discussion of autonomy in language learning and teaching, see Benson, 2007). As Holec (1981) notes, for learners to take charge of their learning, they need to be working within a learning structure that makes this possible. The intention underlying the development of this course was to provide students with opportunities to focus on those aspects of their English language proficiency that they felt needed to be improved. Therefore, the challenge was to create a learning structure that would enable learners to exercise self-direction and take responsibility for their learning while ensuring that they had the requisite metacognitive skills.

CURRICULUM, TASKS, MATERIALS

The course outlined here enables students to create and carry out their own personal learning plans. To do this, it is situated within the framework of a learning structure that transfers key elements of the pedagogy to students. In accordance with Holec's (1981) model of learner autonomy, students become responsible for all aspects of their learning, including determining their goals, choosing materials appropriate for meeting these goals, deciding how they are going to use these materials (e.g., selecting suitable strategies, developing learning activities), monitoring their work and progress on a day-to-day basis, and assessing and evaluating the outcomes.

In addition, there are several other features that define the learning structure. First, students learn primarily through direct access to authentic target language materials, most of which were originally intended for native English speakers rather than for language learners. Second, because learners need to have an optimal amount of time to work on their learning plans, whole-class instruction, which focuses primarily on learning strategies, is limited to 10-minute minilessons delivered at the beginning of each class. Third, learning is personalized. Students decide what they want to learn and proceed at their own pace. They choose materials that they find interesting and work with them in ways that suit their individual learning styles. Fourth, language learning portfolios play an important role in helping learners manage, monitor, and assess their learning. Last but not least, 100% of the final grade is determined through a process of collaborative evaluation based on portfolio assessment. These components that characterize the learning structure have implications for the teacher's role and the physical layout of the learning environment.

In this context, teachers become facilitators and language advisers. Their responsibility is to create a learning environment that provides students with the materials, equipment, tools, guidance, and support they will need in order to successfully develop and carry out their own plan of study. Before the course begins, teachers have to research and assemble learning materials that cater to a wide scope of interests, learning styles, and levels of proficiency. They must organize these materials in a manner that makes them readily accessible. They have to prepare materials that outline strategies for language learning and show students how to use the language materials. Once the course gets underway, teachers spend most of their time working with students individually—or at times in small groups—talking about their learning and offering advice or feedback. In other words, the teacher's role shifts to that of a language adviser who offers students guidance on all aspects of their learning.

In addition to changing the role of the teacher, the learning structure has implications for the physical design of the learning environment. At AIU the course in self-directed language learning is offered in the self-access centre. However, this course could also be offered in a classroom equipped with computers and media players. For teachers interested in establishing a self-access centre, the most comprehensive work to date is Gardner and Miller's (1999) *Establishing Self-Access: From Theory to Practice,* which provides detailed practical information as well as theoretical guidelines. Regardless of where the course is offered, it is important to provide students with a comfortable, relaxed learning environment equipped with a wide range of media and materials.

In the self-access centre, students can choose from a variety of materials, including books (e.g., young adult fiction, short fiction, nonfiction) accompanied by audio recordings, newspapers and magazines, DVDs of movies and television programmes, Test of English as a Foreign Language (TOEFL) materials, computer software, reference books (e.g., grammar books, dictionaries, study guides, screenplays, vocabulary lists), and a selection of English as a foreign language (EFL) listening and reading materials. In designing the learning environment, care has to be taken to display and store the materials in such a way as to attract students' attention and to provide easy access.

Getting Started

To help students select appropriate materials, the course instructors guide them through the process of developing their own learning plans. After an explanation of what self-directed language learning is, students complete a learner profile. Because the main purpose of the profile is to help them focus on their language learning goals, they are asked to think about what they need and want to be able to do in the target language. The profile, therefore, consists of an inventory of things a person can actually do in a language, categorized according to skill (e.g., read newspapers, watch movies, participate in everyday conversations). The students check off the items they feel they need to improve. They then choose three of the checked items that they would like to commence work on immediately.

After students have completed the learner profile, they start work on their personal learning plan (see Appendix A). The learning plan serves two purposes: Apart from structuring the learners' work in the course, it requires them to think about both their learning and how they learn. Providing scaffolding in the form of a series of questions can help guide students through this process. For example, the first item on the form is Goals. Learners should think about the question: What aspects of my English do I need or want to improve? In answering this question, they can refer to their learner profile, where they have already narrowed the possibilities down to three. To simplify the process of developing their first learning plan, students are asked to limit themselves to one goal. Later, they can expand their plan to include more goals. They are also encouraged to state their goals as specifically as possible. For example, rather than "Improve my listening skill," it is better to state the goal more precisely: "Improve listening to everyday conversations." The more focussed the goal is, the easier it is to identify suitable materials and activities.

The next step is for students to select materials that are appropriate for meeting their stated goal. Before they start browsing for materials, they should think about these questions: Which materials will I use to meet my goals? Which materials will help me the most? Which are the most interesting to me? At this point, it is a good idea for the teacher to suggest options for some of the more frequently identified goals and to explain why these materials would be appropriate choices.

Once students have chosen their materials, they need to determine how they will use them for language learning. To complete the Activities/Strategies section on the learning plan, they need to ask themselves some very straightforward questions: How will I use these materials to learn English? What will work best for me? Initially, most of the students choose DVDs or magazines or books with audio recordings. Therefore, during the orientation session, students are offered strategies for using these materials. This is only a starting point. Throughout the course, teachers continue to suggest strategies and model their use in the minilessons delivered at the beginning of each class. Many students will have engaged in out-of-class learning during their high school years and often have their own ideas about how they will use the materials. Other students will adapt the suggestions they are given, and over time a number of students will devise their own strategies. For everybody in the class, this marks the beginning of a period of experimentation, exploration, and reflection on goals, materials, strategies, and their relationship.

Finally, usually weeks later, when students have finished working with the materials or have decided to revise their learning plan, they complete the Assessment section of the learning plan. Here, they record their reflections on the learning experience and note what they learned as a result of having worked with the materials. As in the previous sections, they are asked to consider a series of questions. After students have completed the Assessment section, they then develop a new learning plan.

Once students have created their learning plan and commenced work, they write a language learning history, a personal essay in which they recount the story of how they have learned English (see Appendix B). Near the end of the course, they complete a second assignment in which they write a reflection on the language learning history. In this follow-up assignment, they examine how their views on language learning have changed as a result of the experiences they have had in the course and what they have learned about themselves as language learners. For the students, these assignments have two important purposes. First, they reinforce the idea that a key focus of the course is how students learn English and who they are as language learners. Second, they provide an opportunity for students to consolidate their metacognitive insights. For teachers, not only does the reflection provide insights into students' metacognitive development, but the language learning history offers information about students' identities as learners, which can be helpful when teachers are called on to give advice.

Daily Operation

As soon as students have developed their learning plan, they are ready to go to work. On a typical day, they come to the self-access centre, get their materials, and settle down to work. At the beginning of the class, instructors usually give a 10-minute minilesson. At the end of each class, students have 10 minutes to complete their learning logs and to return materials. As students become accustomed to the routines, the time required for management tasks diminishes.

A key component of the students' day-to-day experience is monitoring their learning. In this context, this means that they keep track of their learning and question the effectiveness of what they are doing in terms of their desired results. Again, scaffolding in the form of questions can offer vital support to learners: Is this material helping me meet my goals? Are my strategies working? What am I learning? How do I know? What do I need to do differently? As a tool to assist in this process, learners maintain a daily learning log (see Appendix C). In their log entries, they note exactly what they did in the class that day, reflect on the experience, and say what they plan to do during the next class. The log plays an important role in helping learners monitor their learning on a regular basis.

Another essential day-to-day responsibility for students is the maintenance of their portfolios. In addition to their daily learning logs, students are encouraged to include other items that provide evidence of their learning (i.e., tangible results of their efforts to develop and use their own assessment strategies). For example, students who have been using TOEFL materials might include score sheets from practice tests, or students who have been working to increase their reading speed might include graphs illustrating their reading times. Research shows that documenting learning in portfolios can enhance learners' awareness of their strategy use and overall metacognitive development (Yang, 2003), but portfolios can also provide the basis for evaluation.

Grading and Assessment Methods

During the final weeks of the semester, students assign themselves an overall grade for the course. Guided by evaluation criteria that focus on language learning as well as learning how to learn a language, students review all the material in their portfolios (learning plans, learning log entries, language learning history and reflection, and other evidence of learning they have accumulated) in order to determine their final grade. They then complete an evaluation report on which they state their grade and explain—in relation to the criteria—why they deserve it. In general, students need to comment on how their language skills might have improved and how they know this as well as what they have learned about how to learn a language. Guided by the same criteria, instructors then review the portfolios and assign grades. If there is a discrepancy, the instructor and the student meet to negotiate an acceptable grade. Should there be a deadlock, the next step is to have a mutually agreed-upon third party review the portfolio, listen to arguments from both sides, and then assign a grade. During the 4 years that the course has been offered, all grading differences have been resolved without the intervention of a third party.

REFLECTIONS

At the end of the course, students complete a course evaluation questionnaire. Each year nearly all of the students indicate that they enjoyed the course. Moreover, their responses support evidence in the portfolios that suggests they developed metacognitive skills, made gains in language proficiency, and experienced high levels of motivation. One student wrote:

> I learned effective ways to learn languages through this course. Now, I can set goals, choose right materials, use effective strategies and evaluate myself. The learning style of this course really motivated me and I did my best to use my time effectively.

Many of the students' comments linked goal setting to enhanced motivation, supporting the claim that setting their own curriculum goals heightens their motivation.

As for gains in language proficiency, it is important to recognize that attributing positive outcomes to this course alone is impossible because of the many intervening variables. Yet the questionnaire responses and evaluation reports indicate that the majority of students were convinced the course had enabled them to improve their language skills. Among other things, students noted increased reading speed, greater ease in communicating with exchange students, and increased comprehension of humour as depicted in movies and television programmes. Students also noted that they had learned about English-speaking cultures and language pragmatics through movies and television programmes.

As they reflected on their learning, a number of students made reference to the combined use of reading and listening skills. They felt that this combination helped them increase their reading speed, improve their listening comprehension, and expand their vocabulary. An additional benefit was that they could do so while using materials they found interesting. The decision to provide students with opportunities to read and listen at the same time to books originally written for native English speakers was based on work done in Canada to create a comprehension-based English as a second language programme for French-speaking public school children (Lightbown, 1992; Mackey, 1991). Research suggests that practising these skills at the same time can even lead to increased oral fluency (Borras & Lafayette, 1994; Lightbown, 1992). Although the issue of combining reading and listening skills in an EFL curriculum bears further empirical investigation, the evidence to date suggests that learners benefit from this strategy.

Another issue pertains to the role of the teacher and control of the learning environment. As a teacher, one of the biggest challenges I faced was relinquishing control of the learning to the learners. Insights provided by Bruner (1996) have helped me realize that, in large measure, my control issues were actually issues of trust related to students' understandings of what was best for them as learners. Bruner maintains that we all possess understandings of how we learn, which he refers to as *folk pedagogy*. He advises educators to first gain an understanding of learners' folk pedagogy and to work from there. Over time, I realized that the starting point for my work with students in this course had to be their understanding of how they learn. My role is to help learners refine and broaden their folk pedagogy by creating a learning structure that offers a variety of learning opportunities, enables learners to expand their repertoire of learning strategies, and encourages them to experiment and critically reflect on what they are doing as well as their progress.

The learning structure outlined in this chapter has also been adapted for adult language learners in a different context. The result is a programme designed to meet the needs of the general public who come to learn English at a self-access centre in the downtown area of Akita City. Learners initially come to an orientation session during which they are guided through the process of setting up their own learning plan. As these learners carry out their plans, they have the possibility of attending advising sessions with language experts and receiving help from learning support staff. The learners at this centre include such groups as businesspeople, housewives, and retired people.

Furthermore, there is evidence to suggest that this learning structure can be modified to meet the needs of young adult language learners. Hale (2006) provides an example of an elective course for Japanese senior high school students that requires them to work in a self-access centre for 1 hour each week over an 8-month period. They have access to graded readers, magazines, newspapers, textbooks, listening programs, and DVDs of movies and television programmes. The students use these materials to pursue their own learning goals.

Regardless of the context in which this learning structure is implemented, it will most likely be new to the students. Lack of familiarity with the mode of learning, combined with their developing English comprehension skills, will make it difficult for students to understand what is expected of them. Mechanisms such as scaffolding and easy-to-use tools such as strategy guides and learning logs have to be built into the structure to ensure that students have the support they need. The learning structure must encompass a variety of elements that enable students to take control of their learning, but the irony is that the structure also imposes controls. The challenge facing teachers is to create a learning structure that maximizes opportunities for learners to take responsibility for the development of their metacognitive and linguistic skills while providing them with the support they require.

Garold Murray is currently developing self-access and e-learning programs at Okayama University, in Japan. Prior to this, he worked at Akita International University, where he established the centre and course discussed in this chapter. His research employs narrative inquiry to explore learner autonomy in language learning in classroom, out-of-class, and self-access contexts.

APPENDIX A: PERSONAL LEARNING PLAN

Name: _____ Date started: _____ Date finished/stopped: _____

Goals:
Materials:

Activities/Strategies: What exactly will you do with this material to help you meet your goals? Please be specific.

Assessment: When you have finished or stopped working with this material, please write about your English learning experience. Ask yourself these questions:

- Did the materials and/or strategies help me meet my goals?

- How do I know—is there any evidence?

- Did I see any language-related learning or improvement?

- How did I check to see if I was learning or improving?

- What would I do differently next time? Did I learn anything about how I learn a language? Other thoughts?

APPENDIX B: LANGUAGE LEARNING HISTORY ASSIGNMENT

Assignment 1: Language Learning History

Write a personal essay in which you tell the story of how you learned English. Here are some suggestions to help you decide what to include in your story:

- When did you first hear English? What kind of impression did it make on you?

- What were your classes like in junior high school and high school? Did you like English then? Why or why not? Do you have any interesting or funny stories to tell that relate to your English language learning?

- When did you decide you really wanted to learn English? What brought this about?

- What things have you done to learn English outside of the classroom?

- Why is learning English so important to you?

- What has been the most effective thing you have done to help improve your English?

- At this point what do you need to do to improve your English? How do you know?

Assignment 2: Reflection on the Language Learning History

1. Reread your essay on your language learning history.

2. Think about the learning experiences you have had in this course. Look at your portfolio. Read the comments you made in the Reflections sections of your daily learning log and personal learning plans.

3. Now write a short essay in which you either

    a) outline how your views on language learning have changed as a result of the experiences you have had in this course and what you have learned about yourself as a language learner

    OR

    b) if your views have **not changed**, explain how the experiences you have had in this course and the things you have learned about yourself as a learner have served to reinforce or confirm the understanding you already had about how you learn a language.

Conclude your reflection by commenting on what you intend to do in order to continue learning English independently after this course.

APPENDIX C: DAILY LEARNING LOG

Daily Learning Log	
Name:	**Date:**
Goals:	
Materials:	
Activities/Strategies (What I actually did):	**Assessment/Reflections** (What I felt/observed):
Planning (What I will do next class):	

CHAPTER 9

Stepping Into a Participatory Adult ESL Curriculum

Sally Lamping

Lamine Kane, a new adult English as a second language (ESL) student, arrived early one evening with a bulging manila folder. "I need some help with this," he stated, and carefully opened the folder.

Within his pile of papers were forms for his wife and two children. It was a familiar family reunification stack—immigration forms and receipts, letters from a lawyer, doctors' records, birth certificates, and money order stubs— but no answers. He pointed to his 4-year-old son's documents.

"I have not been to my country since my son was born. My wife thinks I play some kind of game with her. She does not understand this," he said.

"But this one says 'approved,'" the teacher said eagerly.

Lamine replied, "Yes, and also for my wife and daughter, but they are all approved. I have not heard anything since that time. I have lawyer, but still nothing. My biggest problem is I do not read. I never went to school."

For many adult ESL instructors, meeting the needs of adult language learners like Lamine in the classroom is a complicated task. Limited resources, large class size, and multiple oral and literacy levels often present seemingly insurmountable challenges. By opening classrooms to a participatory approach, however, teachers can help students achieve individualized educational goals within the context of larger and more diverse classrooms with links to the wider community.

The participatory format relates closely to the process syllabus, whereby students and teachers negotiate the learning objectives together and the teacher then creates activities that focus on these objectives (White, 1988). However, participatory classrooms differ in that teachers do not help create objectives for students; instead, through a variety of methods, students create and continually revise objectives for themselves. Because of this, Auerbach (1992) found that participatory classroom outcomes are often unpredictable; however, she writes that such unpredictability "indicates participants have genuinely been involved in determining their objectives" (p. 20). When students self-select objectives, teachers abandon teacher-centered ends-means approaches to the curriculum. Freire

(1983) states that in such an approach, "the teacher is no longer merely the-one-who-teaches, but one who is himself taught in dialogue with students, who in turn while being taught also teach" (p. 67). Participatory educators scaffold the classroom experience by sharing, modeling, preparing environments, and serving as coaches in the attainment of student goals.

This chapter describes a reflective participatory ESL curriculum that recognizes the assets of adult students with limited formal schooling. It outlines a process for investigating and responding to students' needs in a particular classroom community and explains specific participatory components that meet the needs of a diverse adult ESL population.

CONTEXT

In the free adult ESL class operated by the city's public school system, Lamine and his classmates represent an ESL population that continues to grow in U.S. classrooms. Such students could be labeled illiterate, preliterate, underschooled adult ESL, or nonnative adult basic education learners. Working with them, however, forces educators to reconsider literacy labels that focus on deficits. Ferdman (1990) writes that heterogeneous societies similar to the United States must have multiple definitions of literacy. He explains that people who seem unable to access certain texts in one culture may alternately be quite functionally literate in their own culture.

These adult language learners are primarily from countries where public and private schools might teach a written national language, but due to certain life events they have not had access to formal schooling. Although their language is strictly oral, they lived well in their home countries. They are what Ferdman (1990) describes as literate in their own societies. In communities where many interactions require written literacy, however, they struggle daily with multiple obstacles; thus, they appear to have incredible literacy deficits.

Although their lives in the United States are difficult, these students still access employment, health care, housing, and education without written literacy. By simply surviving in the United States, they have fragmented masteries of what Gee (1989) calls discourse: "a sort of 'identity kit' which comes complete with the appropriate costume and instructions on how to act, talk, and often write so as to take on a particular role that others will recognize" (p. 7). Daily interactions in U.S. society force these students to become familiar with dominant U.S. discourse. However, for a variety of reasons, simply understanding this discourse has not been sufficient; they come to school to gain more profound and independent control of their daily lives within this discourse.

Such students choose education because they know the tensions they experience in U.S. society are directly related to their reading and writing skills. For example, a student might repair cars better than his boss, but because he has not passed the General Education Development test, he cannot get his mechanic's license in the United States; therefore, he is underpaid for his skills. As teachers, we know that education cannot erase these tensions, but it can give students the tools to deal critically with them.

Lamine's class operates on open enrollment, and size ranges nightly from 16 to 25 students who have various levels of spoken English skills. The class has one teacher (me) and two native-English-speaking volunteer tutors. To better address student needs in such a context, I consulted five students from the class, who told their stories of immigration and education through a series of taped interviews, focus groups, and informal conversations. They explained how they struggled with the classroom literacy texts but were at ease in groups where they used English to critically discuss their experiences in U.S. society. This consultation made it clear that the students and I needed to choose and implement new classroom practices collaboratively in order to create an individualized participatory framework that made students the focus of the classroom experience. The four components of the developed framework are classroom mentoring, the Individualized Learning Plan (ILP), community meetings, and community forums.

CURRICULUM, TASKS, MATERIALS

Classroom Mentoring

In some countries, mentors or elders serve as guides in several life transitions. Somé (1998) writes that in many African societies, a mentor sees "a presence knocking at a door within the pupil, and accepts the task of finding, or becoming, the key that opens the door" (p. 102). He also denotes that this relationship would be unsuccessful without love and trust. In the case of our ESL class, mentors are fellow nonnative-English-speaking students who might speak the new student's native language, but more important, and unlike their teacher, they have learned to navigate specific parts of U.S. society as newcomers. This classroom mentoring helps build relationships with new students and gives mentors' opportunities to work with language and leadership.

Depending on the classroom context, mentors can assume a variety of roles. As fellow ESL students, they are experts in areas where a new student might have a need. For example, in our class, there are a few mentors who serve as societal brokers. They advise newly arrived students about obtaining immigration documents, social security cards, and driver's licenses; finding local immigrant-friendly employers; pursuing paths to citizenship; and doing grocery shopping. Some mentors are experts in accessing higher education, including enrollment, examinations, and residency procedures, and others know how to obtain workplace-specific documentation such as commercial driver's licenses, certificates for specialized factory work, and trade certifications. In any class, there might be mentors who have purchased cars or houses using loans, opened savings accounts, and learned the best practices for wiring money overseas or using credit. Only those who have had these newcomer experiences understand the nuances of such interactions, so mentors become assets for newly arrived students.

However, participatory classrooms must set up entry points for mentors and new students; otherwise, authentic mentoring relationships would be impossible. In our class, I worked with five consultant students, who later became the first mentors, to develop an easily accessible checklist that identifies initial mentoring procedures. The checklist now serves as a time-saving tool for new mentor orientation. Figure 1 shows an example of a completed mentoring checklist for a student in this class. I added dated notes for record-keeping purposes.

On any evening, a new student can be paired with a suitable mentor in class. Initially, the mentor might discuss the checklist in the student's native language, which allows mentors and students to share specific insider details about the class without feeling pressure to speak English. To avoid overwhelming new students and to ensure classroom practice competency, mentors choose to move through the checklist over the course of a few classes. For example, when a mentor introduces a student to the computers, he or she gives the student an opportunity to practice with the computer language programs (e.g., Rosetta Stone). Thus, dur-

Task		Initials (mentor and student)	
Registration papers		M.D. a.a.	8/23 P. 2 incomplete SL
Student folders		M.D. a.a.	8/25 complete SL
Classroom Library		M.D. a.a.	8/23 complete SL
Restrooms		M.D. a.a.	8/23 complete SL
Computers		M.D. a.a	8/25 complete w/ pract SL
ILP Interview		M.D a.a.	8/28 complete + BEST TEST(i) SL

Figure 1. Mentor Checklist

ing the next class, the student will be able to use the program with little scaffolding. The final item on the checklist is the initial ILP interview, which occurs when the student and mentor complete the acclimation process.

Individualized Learning Plan

ILPs can be created for each student in a class. They include a student's goals for the course; sample activities that students and teachers have selected; and self, peer, and teacher assessments. Students work at their own pace on their ILPs and constantly revise their goals and activities with the help of teachers and mentors. The plans are different in both level and scope for each student, which allows teachers to address individualized needs within the context of a larger classroom. In classes where students have more oral than written language skills, an interview format is an excellent way to create an ILP. Teachers can conduct the interviews with individual students, but an optimal scenario includes the mentor, student, and teacher. When teachers and mentors work together to administer the interview, they place the student at the center of the learning experience. During all interactions with the student, the teacher and mentor work to support the student in achieving his or her goals.

Prior to the ILP interview, the mentor and teacher make adjustments based on previous conversations with the student. The relaxed interview offers the student opportunities to use life stories as one way to fully describe his or her needs. Usually, the teacher reads the questions and, if necessary, the mentor provides clarification for the student. At any time, the student may explain more difficult concepts and stories in his or her native language for the mentor to translate. Usually, the initial interview leads seamlessly into a conversation about ILP goals and tasks. The conversation encourages the student to choose tasks, levels of scaffolding, and conceivable timeframes. But teachers should work with mentors to develop interview questions that are contextually appropriate for their classrooms (see Figure 2). This process helps participatory educators engage in reflective collaborative practice with students.

Initially, some of the questions might appear unrelated to educational goals, but such questions help the teacher and mentor better understand student assets—including family, language, education (formal and informal), and values— without invading the student's personal life. Recording the interview helps the mentor and teacher further discuss progress and ILP goals with students. The only transcribed copy of the interview goes into the student's folder, which holds his or her ILP goals, activities, and resources related to individual learning. Students have full access to their classroom folders, and the mentor, teacher, and student continually revisit the interview to revise student goals.

Classrooms that use mentoring and the ILP as frameworks for curricula are nontraditional contexts. As a result, teachers who seek to implement these practices might have difficulty visualizing their daily applications. Initially assessing student needs, time constraints, and resources is an excellent way to establish

Student Name: _____ Mentor Name: _____

Date: _____ Student's Native Language: _____

1. Tell us a story about how you learned something that you could now teach someone else.

2. Describe "school" in your country.

3. Tell us a story about a time when you struggled in the United States. How did you overcome that struggle?

4. What is difficult for you in the United States?

5. What would you like to understand better about your life here? (Mentor example may be needed.)

6. If you could learn anything today, what would it be?

7. If you could learn anything in the next year, what would it be?

8. One year from now, what do you want to be doing?

9. How can our class help you with # 8?

10. If you had one million dollars, what would you do with it?

Figure 2. Individualized Learning Plan Interview Questions

schedules for other participatory classrooms. Table 1 illustrates a typical evening for this participatory classroom (and a copy of the schedule is attached to each student's folder). Because participatory classrooms are centers of student choice, these activities are optional. Students may choose other options if they do not wish to participate in certain whole-class pieces.

During ILP work, students work alone, in pairs, or in small groups with different levels of assistance. Depending on their plan, students might learn to use the computer, apply for jobs online, or make phone calls to businesses or social service organizations. Other students might review the alphabet, work with basic literacy transcripts, or complete chosen exercises with a tutor. Still other students might take a walk with a tutor or mentor to learn directions, street signs, and neighborhood landmarks. ILP work provides authentic opportunities for students to engage in assisted real-world classroom practice.

Community Meetings

Often, students in ESL classrooms are from cultures that place paramount importance on communities and families. So their deepest concerns lie in the loneliness and lack of community that they often currently feel in the United States. Thus, participatory classroom communities that include such students must celebrate small personal accomplishments. Community meetings remind students of their assets by inviting classroom dialogue. Meeting as a class to share good and bad

Table 1. Sample Schedule

Time	Activity
4:00–5:00	Teacher prepares classroom environment. Students arrive at 5 p.m.
5:00–6:00	Students and mentors work on Individualized Learning Plan (ILP) goals. Teacher and tutors circulate.
6:00–6:15	Community meeting
6:15–6:45	Tiered group activities relating to community meeting OR one-on-one tutoring OR ILP work takes place. New students should note that mentors may not be available during this time.
6:45–7:15	Community forum
7:15–7:30	Community forum debrief
7:30–8:00	ILP self- and peer assessments and conferences

news also allows students to communally celebrate and discuss the tools required to overcome hardship (Auerbach, 1992).

Students with little spoken English might choose to draw pictures and share in their own language for a mentor to translate, other students might share completely in English, and still others might write down their accomplishments and then read them for the class. Students can be encouraged to set goals for community meetings that help them move from drawing pictures to sharing orally in English or writing some words or phrases. In our classroom, students often allow me to record their stories of accomplishment. These recordings can be transcribed and used to make relevant materials for beginning readers whose ILP goals align with the transcripts. This method could be compared to the ever-popular language experience approach that is sometimes used with adult language learners (Wurr, 2002). These activities create trust in the classroom and allow me to once again learn from students' collective stories.

Community meetings can be followed by tiered small-group work in a multi-level classroom. Students can generate activity topics based on dialogue from community meetings. During this time, students might read transcribed pieces from previous community meetings, make conversation cards based on the stories told, write or draw about the topics, or have more focused conversations relating to generative themes (Freire, 1983). Classroom facilitators (anyone who facilitates instruction) can coach by sharing, posing questions, recording observations, and providing feedback on group work.

Community Forums

Because students frequently have issues that are beyond the scope of the classroom, the community forum is a viable participatory component. Together, a class can create a list of topics and possible speakers for the forum. Students then collaboratively choose speakers from this list to research and contact for presentations. Because they are based on student needs, community forums can include a variety of topics. Often, there is an astonishing number of community members, local activists, and former students who are eager to volunteer as speakers. On these particular evenings, students can also invite guests. In our class, the tutors and I coach students in preparing individual questions for the speaker, which increases their personal involvement in the forum. Students who want to attend but who do not have sufficient English language skills to fully understand a speaker sit next to a mentor who quietly translates key points.

Community forums provide opportunities for students to welcome community members into their safe space. On one occasion, a group of students from our class invited their neighborhood police officer to speak. Because of negative police stereotypes in many students' countries and current neighborhoods, several were apprehensive about this forum. Nevertheless, when the lieutenant arrived, shook hands with the students who had invited him, and asked about their lives, the reluctant students relaxed. Unlike the public spaces of their neighborhoods, the classroom was a private safe space where the lieutenant was their invited guest. In turn, they felt free to express their concerns about policing, and the evening was a success. These forums provide students with valuable knowledge and create spaces for student autonomy and leadership.

Self-assessment is an integral part of successful participatory classrooms. At the end of every class, students and mentors can revisit their folders and self-assess. Afterwards, peer and teacher conferences can be used to help revise ILP goals. For newer students, the teacher and tutors need to provide individualized coaching for this activity. Over time, students might need less scaffolding, but it is still important to promote conferencing that helps students reflect on and orally process their own progress.

REFLECTIONS

Two years after joining our program, Lamine fulfilled one personal goal by becoming a U.S. citizen. His family joined him in the United States, and he welcomed a new baby, put his children in school, and became active in his son's kindergarten class. Within the context of his turbulent journey, he also achieved his own goals for literacy: He learned to read and write for his specific purposes, which helped him gain better employment. His classroom environment and self-selected curriculum were among the resources he used to navigate his way through this complicated system.

Participatory adult ESL curricula can provide spaces for underschooled adult students to navigate individual literacy and discourse tensions within diverse classrooms and larger societies. Creating classroom environments that invite student input and use it to create authentic learning experiences requires teachers to be resourceful, highly organized, and continuously reflective. Because all adult ESL students arrive with specific personal educational goals, they are highly responsive to participatory curricula. Moreover, when we as teachers risk becoming coinvestigators in classrooms that examine our worlds, we contextualize the literacy process. Although such curricula are open ended and constantly evolving, they can serve as meaningful models for change.

———————

Sally Lamping began teaching ESL as a Peace Corps volunteer in Guinea-Bissau, West Africa. Upon returning to the United States, she taught high school English and adult ESL in New York City; Washington, DC; and Cincinnati, Ohio. Currently, she is an English education professor at Wright State University, in Dayton, Ohio, in the United States.

CHAPTER 10

Learning Teams in Edinburgh

Olwyn Alexander

Adults reentering formal learning in higher education after a period of employment can be challenging to teach. In committing to an expensive degree course, they may also be losing a regular income and thus tend to take a critical view of a course and its ability to add value to their professional lives. In addition, they may bring with them into the classroom the roles they play in professional contexts (Squires, 1993) and an expectation that they will have some control over what and how they will learn. However, their experience with other educational contexts can lead them to behave in ways that seem to contradict the autonomy of their professional roles. This chapter looks at how adult language learners' professional experience can enhance their studies through the use of learning teams.

People learn naturally by cooperating in groups. In special interest groups, some workplaces, and families, what a person understands and can do is constructed in relation to a community of novice and expert practitioners (Wenger, 1999). Learning arises from the interaction between an individual's current competence and their experience of the world, and it is mediated by conversations with practitioners in the community. This is effectively an apprenticeship model of learning through legitimate peripheral participation (Lave & Wenger, 1991), in which novices have the right to share in and learn from the practices of the community. Learning emerges from conversations between novices and experts or other novices; for example, students can learn from peers whose level of understanding is just above their own or from experts, teachers, or more advanced students who can provide appropriate staging and scaffolding for tasks (Vygotsky, 1978).

A wealth of classroom research (R. Ellis, 2005a; Johnson, Johnson, & Stanne, 2000) has established the benefits of cooperation in groups for learning in general and language learning in particular. However, simply organizing students into groups to do tasks does not guarantee cooperative learning. Group members need to develop a positive attitude towards working together. They have to feel convinced that group tasks are worthwhile, that the goals are achievable, and that each student is able to make a contribution (R. Ellis, 2005a). Teachers should provide training in strategies for effective group cooperation and monitor students' use of these strategies. In addition, groups should be reasonably stable to allow students an opportunity to develop positive interdependence (Johnson, Johnson, & Holubec, 1993). Students from some cultures need a long process of group formation before they feel ready to trust and work with others in a group. Johnson et al. (2000) hypothesize that the effectiveness of cooperative learning tends to increase the more extensively it is built into classroom life. A greater commitment to cooperative learning can be achieved by creating learning teams that share learning goals and function as a stable unit for the duration of a semester or an entire course.

Effective teams interact and share information, value differences among team members, are flexible, and work together to reach desired outcomes. However, failure rates for teams are high (Lick, 2006), often due to lack of commitment and support at an institutional level and the failure of teams to work towards mutually accepted goals with full participation from all team members. Hills (2001) contrasts high-performance teams with learning teams: In the former, individuals who already have good skills use them for the benefit of the team; in the latter, the team comes to recognise what it cannot do and agrees to learn and improve together. In learning teams, members accept that the team goals can further their own learning goals.

For a group of individuals to become a team, they must go through a natural process of team formation in which they learn how to function together. The process is often referred to as *forming-storming-norming,* which is followed by *performing.* Storming is a stage of constructive conflict (Katzenbach & Smith, 1993) in which team members realise the scope of their task and question whether they can achieve it. Very little task learning might be happening, but the team is developing interpersonal skills. Costello, Brunner, and Hasty (2002) suggest that students preparing for the uncertainty of the workplace need a learning environment where neither questions nor answers are clearly defined. Team learning tasks scheduled during the storming stage can create such an environment by containing a degree of ambiguity that requires negotiation to understand the requirements of a task and how these can be shared. Resolving this ambiguity can help build team commitment.

CONTEXT

The teaching context is a Research Skills module delivered at Heriot-Watt University, in Edinburgh, Scotland, as part of an MSc in Strategic Project Management. This module enrolled 25 adult language learners with a range of diverse backgrounds. They were all nonnative speakers of English with advanced language proficiency, and most had more than 2 years' work experience and high expectations of the module. The majority had experience doing research at work or university, and most said they felt confident working in teams.

Team working is now a significant component of many workplaces (Hills, 2001; Lick, 2006), and most workplace projects are managed by teams. To simulate this practice during the module, students were organised into learning teams using a series of self-perception tests (Belbin, 1993) that attempted to assess the type of contribution each person was likely to make to a team. The aim was to achieve a balance in the teams. Most modules in the programme include one team assignment in addition to individual coursework.

The Research Skills module aimed to present the academic culture, language, and skills needed to carry out research for a thesis using an experiential learning approach. Students gained direct experience with the research process by carrying out a small research project in which they read about a topic and chose an aspect that interested them. They identified a context (e.g., a company they have worked for) where they would be able to collect data and decided which of the theoretical concepts they were studying could be applied to the data. Following this, they designed a research question and wrote a proposal. They then collected and analysed the data and presented their findings in a report. The module was delivered through a series of workshops designed to familiarise students with the texts they have to read and write at each stage of the process. There was no explicit language teaching. Instead, students were presented with a series of tasks that required them to use language and skills for research.

CURRICULUM, TASKS, MATERIALS

The Research Skills module was taught jointly by an instructor skilled in team learning and an English for academic purposes (EAP) instructor (the author). Student teams received input on effective team working and the importance of goal setting, sharing tasks, and communicating. A sample exercise (from Hills, 2001) invited all team members to write down at least one skill they have that they were prepared to share and one they would like to learn. Team members then compared their skills and identified learning opportunities in the team.

Teams were required to prepare a team contract specifying how they would work and learn together. To be explicit about the fact that each team was responsible for how effectively its members worked together, students were told that they were free to write the contract as the team saw fit but could consider using the following headings: team name, introduction (which might include learning opportunities identified in the previous exercise), aims and objectives, decision making, expectations about work quality, communication, confidentiality, conflict and disputes, commitment and personal accountability. For all team assignments, each team was required to analyse how it carried out the tasks and write an assessment of how the team was functioning. Figure 1 shows a series of questions that can be used to prompt reflection about the effectiveness of team working.

The students were given questionnaires at the beginning and end of the module to evaluate its content and delivery, including how well team learning worked for them personally and how they thought it could be improved. As part of their final submission, each student wrote a reflective statement outlining what he or she had learned. Many students commented on team working in these documents. The team contracts and analyses, together with student evaluations, reflective statements, and instructor observations, were used to follow the process of learning in teams as the course proceeded.

The task chosen as the team assignment for the Research Skills module was the preparation of an annotated bibliography. This came at the point in the research process where students were reading about their chosen topic and trying to choose an aspect that interested them. The assignment was intended to encourage them to read in a focused way and to learn how to categorise and evaluate the sources they were reading. The task required that they work together to negotiate a topic for the bibliography and share the task of finding and reviewing a range of relevant sources. Then each student had to select from these sources to prepare an individual bibliography. This was to consist of a brief introduction to set the context and a list of at least 10 sources relevant to the topic, with a paragraph-length annotation evaluating the scope, relevance, and usefulness of each source. The task was viewed as a formative exercise to encourage team working. The bibliographies were given an individual grade and feedback, so there was no team component beyond the negotiation of the topic.

Does your team know what its learning goals are?

Does your team know how each member's individual learning goals fit with the team's learning goals?

Does everyone in your team think that he or she has something to contribute, and do you know what that is?

Have you checked that each member of your team understands the objectives of a team assignment?

How good is your team at planning together? Is there a lot of confusion or duplication of effort?

Does everyone in your team feel able to have his or her say? Do you have any mechanisms for ensuring that everyone's voice is heard?

Does everyone in your team feel able to evaluate individual and joint successes and failures and talk freely about these?

Can you identify any tensions in your team, either positive or negative?

Do you have a way of dealing with any negative tensions?

Figure 1. Questions to Encourage Evaluation of Team Working

Student Responses to Team Working

The students were divided into teams of five. Some students adapted quickly to team working, and their teams prepared detailed contracts stating the aims of the team and agreeing how they would cooperate, take responsibility for tasks, and manage disagreement. Other students were slower to accept team working. Their team contracts were brief, with goals and some rules for working together. Only one team did not prepare a contract. Students in this team acknowledged in the analysis for their first team assignment that they had not worked effectively as a team. They seemed unwilling to take responsibility for working together or dealing with conflict and instead criticised the way the teams were set up and the fact that they had to work with the same team throughout the term.

Those students who found team working to be a positive learning experience said that it had given them an opportunity to learn about other cultures and improved their ability to communicate, share ideas, and develop team working skills. Some contracts explicitly specified these team goals, for example, to "ensure the effectiveness of the team and learning chance for everybody" and "develop better learning and working relationship between members of the group." The analysis of their first team assignment referred back to these goals and, in one case, described how the team was able to "draw strength from our individual differences." This team reported that once they had clarified the scope of the team assignment, this "greatly increased team morale."

When commenting on whether they had functioned as expected from their team roles and what insights they had gained, several students said that setting up teams in a formal way using self-perception tests (Belbin, 1993) was a new experience that they did not consider to be particularly accurate. More than half said their profile indicated more than one team role or that they functioned in different ways at different times. However, a number commented that their team role gave them good insight into their behaviour in teams.

Student Responses to the Team Assignment

The team assignment for Research Skills is due early in the semester, so it probably coincides with the storming stage when teams are learning to work together and are uncertain whether they will be able to achieve the task. Producing an annotated bibliography may seem to be a relatively simple task, and the shared search for and evaluation of sources should have helped reduce the effort for each individual. However, the task requires teams to negotiate how they will cooperate, to discover that their personal learning goals may not match the team goals, and to decide what to do about this.

In four of the five teams, the assignment created some conflict because students wanted to work on different topics and found it difficult to negotiate a team topic that interested them all. In their evaluations, some students suggested that the instructions for the annotated bibliography were unclear and they needed better direction about how to work on this assignment. Many students were unable to focus the topic sufficiently, a recurring problem for research, and produced bibliographies with little connection between the sources. More effective team working might have provided these students with a critical audience for their work. Several students admitted that they had not taken the task seriously but said that feedback from me, the EAP instructor—and a low grade—helped change this attitude. Others appeared to hold me responsible for their difficulties. However, one student commented specifically in her reflective statement about the usefulness of the assignment:

> The process of finding sources, reading, selecting and evaluating the sources was lengthy and painful. I had never read articles and books that thoroughly before. However, it was worthwhile. While it took one week to complete the annotated bibliography, it took only two days to write [the other] assignment, which was amazing compared to my normal one or two weeks on similar essays.

REFLECTIONS

As it stands, the task described in this chapter introduces ambiguity and a useful tension between the negotiated team topic and individual interests, which the teams must try to resolve. However, it was clear from the team conflicts that arose that many students did not view the annotated bibliography as a team task. For example, it can be completed without a mutually shared and accepted goal, the topic, and without full participation of all team members, and grades are given to individuals, not to the team, with no penalty for noncooperation.

In reviewing the module, I proposed making the annotated bibliography a team submission, but the course director thought it would be more useful as an individual submission to encourage students to begin reading early to discover areas of research that interested them. He suggested that the team aspect could be strengthened by requiring teams to peer review each team member's bibliography (see Appendix).

This module has provided insights that can inform the use of learning teams in other contexts where adult language learners have high expectations of a course. The generic features of the course described here are that it involves a process with well-defined tasks at each stage and each task outcome is a written document with a conventional format. One or more of the tasks requires team cooperation. These features could be transferred to contexts in which teamwork is routine, for example, engineers or architects working on design projects, construction managers leading teams on building sites, or nurses and social workers dealing with case studies. Learning teams could be used to improve business communication, for example, between management and employees or among international partners. Those familiar with team working can learn to work more effectively as a result of reflecting on their performance in team tasks. The students in this module ultimately responded well to the opportunity to experience an environment where not everything is specified in advance but aspects are ambiguous or messy and negotiable and the teacher does not have all the answers. These circumstances correspond more closely to their workplace experience and encourage them to take responsibility for their learning.

It is important to have a clear and continuing commitment to team working and to formalise this with team contracts and a team-assessed exercise. Teams should be set up to contain a mix of preferred ways of working and learning amongst team members, and there should be an awareness-raising exercise in which they reflect on how differences in individual styles might affect team working and communication. Although knowledge of their team roles helped these students reflect on their contribution to the team, Hills (2001) suggests that it is not necessary to use such specific tools and that a learning styles questionnaire could perform the same function. However, he warns against reinforcing learning styles, saying that flexibility and willingness to try different learning styles promotes more effective team working.

Team tasks should be structured to ensure that they really contain shared goals that require full participation from team members, with penalties for not contributing, and that there is scope to provide feedback on team working. However, it is also important to consider what phase the team is going through when it carries out a task. During the team formation phase, simple tasks such as the annotated bibliography assignment reported here can provide learning opportunities for teams. Support in the form of guided reflection enables individuals to see that they learn more from working in teams than they do from working alone.

Olwyn Alexander is a teaching fellow at Heriot-Watt University, in Edinburgh, Scotland. She teaches academic writing and research skills to postgraduate students and is involved in the development of online materials for academic English courses in applied sciences, engineering, and management. Her research interests include team learning and teacher education.

APPENDIX: PEER FEEDBACK ON ANNOTATED BIBLIOGRAPHY

Criteria for Assessing This Assignment	Yes	Sometimes	No
Is the topic of the bibliography sufficiently focused and the level appropriate?			
Does the assignment have an introduction that clearly sets the context and audience for the bibliography?			
Is there a focused question or purpose stated in the introduction?			
Does the introduction support its claims by referring to the work of other writers and acknowledging these?			
Does the choice of references relate clearly to the specified purpose?			
Are the references listed using a recognised convention?			
Do the annotations describe and evaluate using some of the aspects specified in the task?			
Do the annotations relate to each other so a new researcher has an idea of where to start reading?			
Are the annotations detailed and comprehensive?			
Do the annotations seem to be in the writer's own words?			
Is the language largely free of basic errors?			

CHAPTER 11

An Interactive Approach to Book Reports

Melvin R. Andrade

The benefits of graded readers, especially for extensive reading, are well documented. Among them are improvements in fluency, motivation, writing, vocabulary, and attitude toward learning a foreign language (e.g., Day & Bamford, 1998; Krashen, 1993). By using graded readers, students learn to read for pleasure as well as information and develop a sense of reading as a lifelong habit. In addition to developing reading skills, graded readers serve as a basis for follow-up speaking and writing activities. Typically, these activities include a book report in which students present a summary and opinion of what they read. With increasing use of the Internet, however, plagiarism has become a growing problem (e.g., Australian Universities Teaching Committee, 2002). Students can easily find summaries and discussions of books they have read and just as easily copy and paste this information into their own reports. This chapter describes one way of transforming the common book report into an interactive, integrated skills project that has the added benefit of making plagiarism more difficult.

CONTEXT

There has been increasing interest in using graded readers to engage students more fully in the learning experience and to achieve balanced, integrated learning in reading, writing, speaking, and listening. Bamford and Day (2004) describe more than 100 activities that teachers have used to make extensive reading with graded readers and other materials an important component of their language curriculum. Publishers of graded readers, such as Penguin, Macmillan, and Oxford, describe numerous activities in their teacher guides and resource articles as well (e.g., Dawson, 2005; Walker, 2001). In addition to extensive reading, Furr (2007) advocates using graded readers for intensive or semi-intensive reading in reading circles to deeply engage readers with the text through collaborative interaction with their classmates.

Graded readers are wonderful at motivating students and building confidence when the focus is on the reader's personal interaction with the book. That is, students "construct their own meaning by connecting the textual material to issues in their lives and describing what they experience as they read" (Annenberg Media, 1997–2009, ¶ 6). By visualizing and reflecting on the contents, students can go beyond merely comprehending information to experiencing the text more deeply (Appleton, 2004). Furthermore, encouraging students to explore their own thinking and feelings about what they have read leads them to trust their own responses in group discussions rather than depending on the teacher to play a controlling role as the "expert."

The Japanese students that I teach are English majors in their first or second year of university. All have had six years of previous experience learning English, starting in junior high school, and are assigned to courses based on ability level. The students in the lowest level course are in the Test of English for International Communication range of 200–300, and those in the upper level courses are in the 400–500 range. The graded readers are used in integrated skills courses for listening, speaking, reading, and writing.

CURRICULUM, TASKS, MATERIALS

Graded readers are typically divided into six or seven levels of difficulty, ranging from about 200 to 3,000 headwords. For lower ability first-year students, the initial goal is to wean them away from the slow, intensive reading based on translation that many of them used in high school. Accordingly, to build confidence and fluency and a positive attitude toward reading, students can start with books at Level 2 or 3, which can be finished quickly, usually one book a week. Normally for higher level books, students write two or three reports for each one. Each report covers a different section of the book. Writing book reports in this way makes plagiarism more difficult because students are unlikely to find a summary or opinion that exactly fits the section of the book they read that week. Students read without the assistance of the teacher (except for individual questions about the contents or language of the book), but the amount of assistance and time needed to finish a book varies depending on the individual student or level of the class.

The core task is an interactive book report that consists of three main parts: a summary, an opinion or reaction statement, and a short quotation from the book along with the reason for choosing it. In addition, the students prepare their own short quiz covering the contents of their summary and opinion. Model book reports and reports written by students in previous courses are studied so that current students become familiar with the format. In addition, there are three optional activities: doing a self-evaluation, creating a slideshow, and compiling descriptive statistics of their reading performance.

Format of the Book Report

Summary

A summary is an essential component of any book report. Depending on the level of the class and the length of the book, these summaries can range from about 200 to 300 words or more. Students begin by stating the bibliographic information. Next, for fiction books, they describe the setting and main characters and briefly outline the plot. For nonfiction books, students identify the number of main ideas, briefly describe them, and state the conclusion. To guide their summary writing, it is helpful to provide guiding questions and models (see Table 1).

Opinion

This section is roughly equal in length to the summary, but students have more freedom to express their opinions or other reactions to the book. Again, guiding questions are helpful for stimulating writing and discussion (see Figure 1). As a general rule, the opinion is written in paragraph form, not in a question-and-answer format, and students do not need to answer all questions. Handing out examples of model opinions, explaining paragraph structure, and teaching the use of transition expressions (e.g., *however, in addition, for example, moreover, therefore*) will, of course, improve the quality of students' writing.

Short Quotation

Choosing an interesting or important quotation can help the reader engage more deeply with the text and provide a taste of the author's style and the book's tone. To choose a meaningful quotation, students have to consider the book (or chapter) as a whole and then explain the reason for choosing it. The questions in Figure 1 can also be used to select quotations.

Table 1. Questions and Prompts for Summary Writing

Fiction	Nonfiction
Who are the main people in the story?	This book is about . . .
When did the story happen?	There are (insert number of) main ideas.
Where did the story happen, or what places is it concerned with?	First, (main idea 1) + (detail or example).
	Second, (main idea 2) + (detail or example).
What is the story about?	Third, (main idea 3) + (detail or example).
How did the story begin?	The conclusion is . . . .
What happened after that?	
How did the story end?	

What did you think of the book?

What do you think is the theme of this book (e.g., the importance of friendship)?

What did you find interesting, surprising, shocking, or strange?

What other feelings did you have when you read this book?

How does it compare to your life?

How does it compare to your country?

What is something new that you learned?

What do you agree or disagree with in the story?

Have you changed your ideas about anything because of reading this book?

What more would you like to know about this topic?

What do you predict will happen?

If you were a character in the story, what would you have done differently?

If you were the author, would you change anything in the book?

Would you recommend this book to others? Why?

Figure 1. Questions for Guiding Opinion Writing

Presenting the Book Report in Class

Book reports are presented in class in small groups of about four students each. This procedure is flexible; steps may be added, deleted, or modified to suit the circumstances (see the Appendix for a brief outline of this procedure).

Step 1: Summary

The book report writer presents the summary by reading aloud, following an oral presentation template, using notes or speaking from memory. As the book report is presented, the other students in the group take notes using a worksheet to record the bibliographic details and information about the setting, characters, and main events in the story. If parts of the presenter's summary are incomprehensible, then the listeners can ask for sections to be repeated so that they can complete their note-taking tasks. Thus, interaction often occurs as listeners ask the speaker to slow down, speak more loudly, repeat, or rephrase unknown words so that they do not miss important information. This feedback is an effective way to make presenters aware of their audience when speaking.

One way to introduce note taking is to demonstrate the process: As one student orally presents a book report, the teacher writes on the board, following the same format as the worksheets. After students become familiar with note taking, they can progress from using worksheets to using blank sheets.

Step 2: Reply to Questions

During this step, listeners have an opportunity to complete and confirm the accuracy of their notes. They ask information questions (who, what, where, when, why, and how) to fill in missing details and check the correctness of what they have written by retelling the information: "You said . . . . Is that right?" This step also lets the speaker know how effectively he or she was able to communicate.

Step 3: Quiz on the Summary

Another way to keep the listeners involved is to quiz them on the content of the summary and opinion. Moreover, having the book report writers prepare their own quizzes makes them aware of the importance of writing and presenting their summary and opinion clearly and coherently so that listeners can understand and remember what is said. A typical quiz might consist of a few true/false questions, a few multiple-choice comprehension questions, a few vocabulary questions, and perhaps a few open-ended comprehension questions. These quizzes are given in a lighthearted manner, more like a game than a test, and students mark their own answers. The teacher does not grade the results.

Step 4: Opinion

The book report writer presents the opinion by either reading aloud or speaking from memory. As in Step 1, listeners engage in active listening by taking notes using a worksheet.

Steps 5 and 6: Reply to Questions, Short Quiz

As in Step 2, the book report writer replies to questions and then presents a short quiz. However, the second quiz, which deals with an opinion rather than a summary, does not have to adhere to exactly the same format, number of items, or types of questions as the first one.

Step 7: Short Quotation

As in Steps 1 and 2, the book report writer presents the short quotation and engages the listeners by asking about their reaction to it.

Step 8: Discussion

At this point, the speaker and listeners talk about the story and share opinions. They compare the story to their own lives and the situation in their own country. They can ask each other, for example, what they would have done if they were a character in the story or how they would change the ending if they were the author. It may be helpful to remind students how to use conditionals (e.g., "If I were the author, I would have . . .").

Step 9: Exchange Journals

Students exchange journals or papers, read each other's book reports, and write comments and questions to their partners. Depending on the time available, students exchange journals with one or more partners in their group. Students who were not able to follow the oral presentations now have a chance to read the parts that they missed.

Step 10: Self-Evaluation

At the end of each class, students complete a self-evaluation questionnaire about their participation in group discussions. Monitoring their own behavior in this way helps students develop their metacognitive skills and enhance their learning strategies. Moreover, by keeping a personal record of what they have done and how well they have done it, students learn to judge for themselves where their strengths and weakness are. Teachers can modify the contents and scoring to fit the needs and aims of their courses.

Step 11: Slideshow Presentation

This step is optional. If the class has access to presentation software, students can engage in a creative project in which they present their book reports to the entire class using images as well as text. After watching each presentation, audience members can fill out a feedback sheet to give to each presenter. It can be a simple form asking for "good points of the presentation" and "suggestions for improvement," or it can be more detailed, covering categories such as delivery, organization, and content.

Step 12: Descriptive Statistics

At the end of the semester, students usually find it interesting to produce charts and graphs representing their reading performance in class. It is not too difficult to teach basic spreadsheet operations so that students can produce bar graphs and line charts to graphically display the number of words or pages they read each week, their reading rate, and the results of their self-evaluation questionnaires or presentation feedback sheets. Keeping track of how much work they are doing and how well they think they are doing it can aid in teaching students how to be self-directed, aware learners. Furthermore, having this data makes it easier to discuss student performance at the end of the term during one-on-one consultations. This step, of course, is optional and depends on availability of computers and software.

REFLECTIONS

Questionnaire results at the end of the semester have consistently indicated the popularity of graded readers and interactive book reports. Students appreciate the variety of content and enjoy discussing their opinions and exchanging journals with each other. However, as the semester progresses and students begin reading longer or high-level graded readers, it is necessary to lengthen the deadlines for finishing the book reports. Pushing students to do too much too fast—even with lower level readers—may create dissatisfaction.

The interactive book report described in this chapter incorporates several of R. Ellis's (2005a) 10 general principles for successful instructed learning. In this regard, the interactive book report should have wide application in a variety of English as a foreign and second language settings. Specifically, it contributes to focus on meaning, extensive second language input, opportunity for output, and opportunity to interact in the second language. In addition, it accounts for individual differences by allowing students to choose materials that fit their ability level and interests. Although graded readers may not be the material of choice for some programs, the instructional procedure described in this chapter can apply to other types of reading material as well.

Melvin R. Andrade has an EdD from the University of California, Berkeley, and is a professor of English education and applied linguistics at Sophia Junior College, in Japan. His primary research interests are computer-assisted language learning, content-based language teaching, and English for academic purposes. He has taught English in the United States and Japan.

APPENDIX: BOOK REPORT ORAL PRESENTATION GUIDE

Step	What the Speaker (Book Report Writer) Does	What the Listeners Do (Examples)
1	Gives a summary of the book	Take notes using graphic organizers, outlines, timelines, fill-in tables, or other techniques
2	Replies to the listeners' questions	Retell: "You said . . . . Is that right?" Ask questions: who, what, where, when, why, how
3	Gives an oral quiz about the contents of the summary	Take the quiz, respond one by one in turn

4	Gives an opinion or reaction	Take notes using graphic organizers, outlines, timelines, fill-in tables, or other techniques, as in Step 1
5	Replies to the listeners' questions	Retell: "You said . . . . Is that right?" Ask questions: who, what, where, when, why, how
6	Gives an oral quiz about the contents of the opinion	Take the quiz, respond one by one in turn, as in Step 3
7	Reads a short quotation from the book and explains why it is important, interesting, surprising, etc.	Respond with comments or questions
8	Asks the listeners for comments and opinions about the topics or events in the book	Relate the contents to their personal life, compare the situation to their country, etc.
9	After all members of the group have finished presenting, they exchange journals, read their partner's book reports, and write comments.	
10	Complete a self-evaluation questionnaire about their participation in the group discussion	
11	*End of the semester:* Presents a slideshow about one of the books.	Fill out a feedback sheet evaluating the presentation
12	*End of the semester:* Prepare charts of their performance (reading rate, number of pages read, scores on the self-evaluation questionnaire, feedback results, etc.)	

CHAPTER 12

A Web of Controversy: Critical Thinking Online

Joseph V. Dias

What do smoking in public places, eating disorders, performance-enhancing drugs, domestic violence, and animal experimentation have in common? They all generate an enormous amount of heat in the media and are the focus of countless Web pages, newsgroups, and mailing lists. They are also representative of topics that students have selected for in-depth research in the course that this chapter describes. The course was designed to promote language development, academic research, employment, and citizenship skills. With a focus on researching controversial issues through Internet sources, university English majors in Japan move from a vague affinity for an issue to an intimate knowledge of it and identification with its key players. These adult language learners are called on to exercise autonomy at every stage. They select an issue and hold their own in a team that they form to investigate it, thereby becoming accountable citizens of the Web and of the world.

CONTEXT

A Web of Words: Controversy on the Internet is a course that has been offered in various manifestations to sophomores in the Integrated English (IE) Program of the English Department at Aoyama Gakuin University since 1997. It was originally conceived to familiarize students with online resources and to give them an opportunity to carry out project-based international exchanges. Mantovani (1996) has noted that

> as soon as a technology reaches the degree of maturity and reliability that really makes it usable, attention switches from the technological aspects of artifacts—which were previously difficult to master and therefore of great concern for non-specialist users—to the activities, projects and goals of social actors using artifacts for their own purposes. (p. 2)

This having been the case with computer and Internet technology over the past decade, the course organically evolved into one primarily concerned with researching controversial issues. The latest incarnation of the course challenges and stretches students' linguistic and academic abilities while providing a context for purposeful use of Web resources. Despite advances in the technical competence of adult language learners, they often require as much guidance in judging the validity of online sources as younger learners. Therefore, I offer suggestions later in the chapter on criteria for judging online information.

CURRICULUM, TASKS, MATERIALS

In addition to the desired outcome of developing citizenship skills, information literacy is another key aspect of this course, especially Web-specific information literacy because students these days instinctively turn to the Web for their information needs. Pizzorno (2006), who describes an information literacy course for adult English as a second language (ESL) learners in California, points out how "the Internet has replaced . . . traditional research tools and now acts as a virtual library where students can access much of the information they need to complete academic tasks" (p. 263). Such engagement with technology-supported, purposeful tasks represents an embodiment of what has been referred to as *sustained-content language teaching* (SCLT; Ponder & Powell, 2001), which Pizzorno saw as the methodology behind his course as well. SCLT usually involves a focus on a particular theme for at least a term and aims to integrate that content with the four skills and "cognitive and metacognitive strategies; study skills; and the development of vocabulary, grammar, and pronunciation, among other areas" (J. M. Murphy & Stoller, 2001, p. 3).

Unlike Pizzorno's (2006) course, in which information literacy was the content area, the course described in this chapter has controversial issues as the content and language skills and information literacy are cultivated as a means to accomplish the real-world responsibilities of finding out about, caring about, and possibly doing something about a particular social issue of consequence. At the outset of the semester, students are told that due to collaboration on assignments and group projects, regular class attendance is essential. The many artifacts produced in each phase of the seminar—blogs, surveys, Web sites or podcasts, concepts for nongovernmental organizations (NGOs)—all figure into final grades. Because the blogs show the fruits of students' research and should represent the most significant input of time and energy, they are given the greatest weight. Self-assessments and peer assessments are used for the evaluation of Web sites and podcasts.

Shopping for a Cause

After being introduced to controversial issues, students search for one that they feel can sustain their enthusiasm for an entire semester. The Web sites of many university libraries offer excellent annotated lists of controversial issues, but those found in search engine directories or on Wikipedia are likely to be more up to date. Although Wikipedia can be useful for exposure to a wide variety of issues (*Category:Controversies*, 2008), students need to be made aware that it should not be relied upon for academic research.

An intake survey at the beginning of the seminar each year has consistently shown that few students have had experience using mailing lists or newsgroups. Because these tools will be used later in the course, an offline simulation is conducted to help students become familiar with how they function, to explore preliminary controversial issues, and to identify possible collaborators. A form is distributed to students who identify a controversial issue as the main discussion topic in this offline discussion (see Figure 1).

At this point, students need not commit themselves to researching the issue in depth. They write a message expressing their stance and invite contributors to the

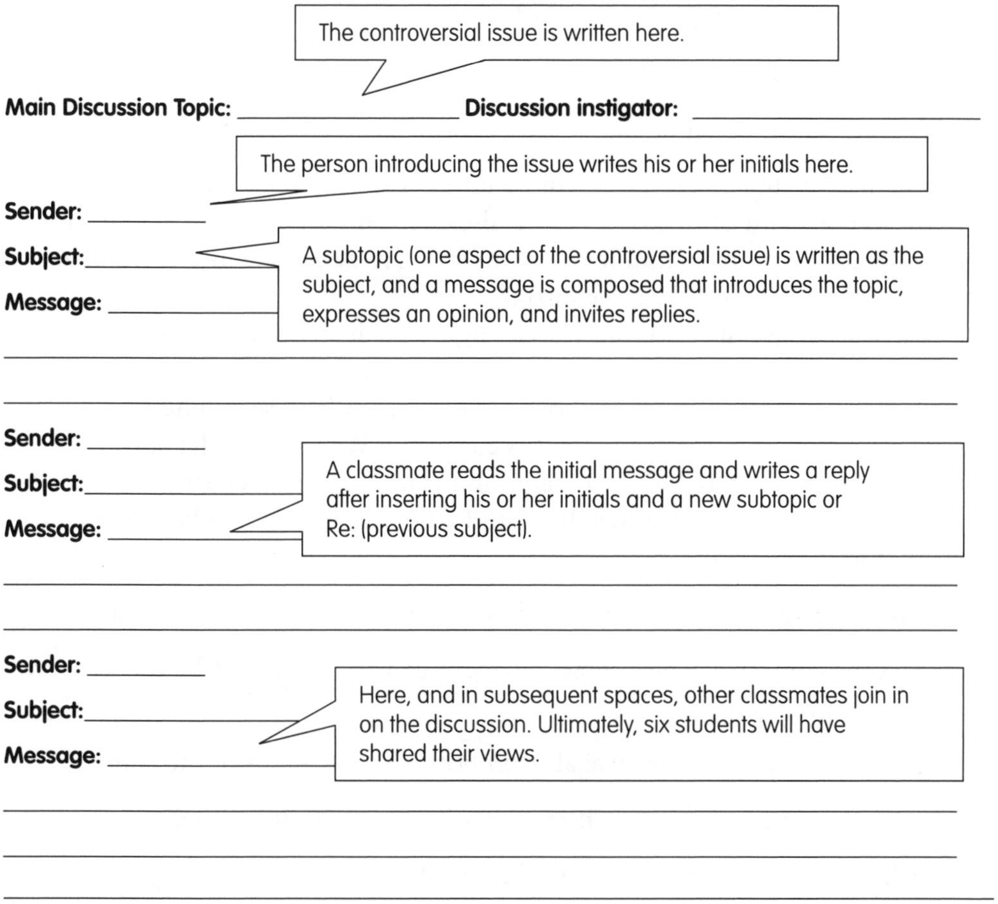

The controversial issue is written here.

Main Discussion Topic: _____ **Discussion instigator:** _____

The person introducing the issue writes his or her initials here.

Sender: _____

Subject: _____

Message: _____

A subtopic (one aspect of the controversial issue) is written as the subject, and a message is composed that introduces the topic, expresses an opinion, and invites replies.

Sender: _____

Subject: _____

Message: _____

A classmate reads the initial message and writes a reply after inserting his or her initials and a new subtopic or Re: (previous subject).

Sender: _____

Subject: _____

Message: _____

Here, and in subsequent spaces, other classmates join in on the discussion. Ultimately, six students will have shared their views.

Figure 1. Offline Discussion About Preliminary Controversial Issue

discussion. Students circulate around the room, adding their input to the discussion sheets until they are full. For homework, the initiators of each discussion summarize the exchanges on a class message board. The following is an example of a particularly well-encapsulated discussion on the pros and cons of zoos:

> I started out with a neutral message hoping to get opinions from both sides. Some think that it's cruel to keep animals in cages, and that it is better for them to live in their natural habitat. . . . I think zoos have their pros and cons, and I'm torn in between because as much as I love seeing animals from different parts of the globe, it's quite saddening to see them in such small confinements.

In the next stage of the task, students try to persuade their classmates—either online or through in-class discussions—to join a research team dealing with the issue introduced in their offline discussions. Here are a few examples of persuasive expressions that can be offered as prompts:

- This issue is important because . . .

- If something is not done about _____, then . . .

- We should do something to stop/reform _____ because . . .

- Won't you join me to find out what can be done about _____?

- Let me tell you a bit about _____ so you can see how important it is.

Naturally, for students to be recruited into a research team, it is necessary for one-half to one-third of the topics to be discarded. Although this is easy for the uncommitted, it can be painful for students who are genuinely interested in a topic but fail to convince their classmates.

A particularly useful clustering search engine, such as *Clusty* (Vivisimo, 2004–2009), is recommended as a way to help students map out the semantic domains of their issues and identify opposing camps. When searching for "bullying," for example, the search engine lists clusters of Web sites under such categories as "dealing with bullies," "parents and teachers," and "cyber bullying." Here are some questions that may help students structure their solicitations for collaborators:

- Are there opposing sides? [Show that the issue is really controversial.]

- Has the controversy been precisely identified? [It shouldn't be too general or too specific.]

- Is sufficient information available on both—or all—sides of the issue?

- Can the topic sustain your interest until the end of the course?

- Why are you personally interested in this topic?

Once the groups have been formed, the in-depth research into the controversial issues begins. As an aid to processing the information uncovered on the issue through various online sources, groups learn how to create and maintain a blog. The free blog-hosting site *Blogger* (Google, 1999–2009) can be used for this purpose, but other options have more flexibility, such as the open source *WordPress* (n.d.) or university-wide systems such as Blackboard (see Blackboard, 1997–2009). With these vehicles, students can demonstrate that they are struggling to come to terms with their issue by summarizing, synthesizing, and analyzing relevant information. Students are provided with a checklist that clearly delineates the requirements and individual responsibilities, which may include parameters for the length of entries, a stipulation that students must consult a variety of reference and news sources (e.g., online dictionaries, encyclopedias, podcasts, and possibly videos), and the necessity for commenting on each others' blogs to provide useful feedback and to ensure an appreciative audience.

Creating Criteria for Judging Online Information

Students can better understand the essential criteria for evaluating Web sources after being called on to locate and present to the class one Web site related to their issue that they feel is trustworthy and another that is suspicious. They are then asked to identify which features of the Web sites account for their trust or distrust. Although a few prompts will be needed, several phrases might be suggested to orient students to key issues: *well written, up to date, widely respected, user friendly, nonjudgmental.* Sentence prompts might also be offered: "I can generally trust Web sites that . . ." or "I tend to (dis)trust Web sites that have/offer . . ." or "I would absolutely avoid Web sites that . . . ." Usually, in a class of 25–30 students, a list of criteria can be generated that is superior to those listed in books or journals (e.g., Clankie, 2000; Thiroux, 1999, pp. 64–70) and to the ones provided on Web sites that offer guidance in assessing the quality of Internet sources (see Appendix A).

In addition to items on their criteria lists, such as "good" sites having balanced information and known authorship, students often come up with unique criteria that make perfect sense for English language learners. For example, one recent group of students identified trustworthy sites as having bilingual support, an unambiguous perspective, and English that is appropriate to their level of ability, whereas untrustworthy sites lacked graphics to support the meaning of texts, were not constructive (overly cynical, personal, sarcastic, or unfairly critical), and offered a great deal of raw data without commentary to put it into context.

Creating an Online Survey

A goal of the course is to empower students so that they can create and not just consume information. They do this through their ongoing blogging and also by creating surveys on their controversial issue using the free mode of *SurveyMonkey*

(SurveyMonkey.com, 1999–2009), an online survey hosting service. Students are able to gain valuable practice in composing a variety of question types: yes/no, multiple choice, and open ended. They may also learn how to make polite requests (e.g., for soliciting participants), organize items in a logical way, and, after the results are in, summarize results graphically and in writing. Before the surveys are promoted more widely, classmates from other groups take them and evaluate their quality using a checklist (see Appendix B). This feedback helps students revise their surveys.

Once the surveys are made presentable, students seek out mailing lists and newsgroups where they are likely to find potential respondents. They can look on *Yahoo! Groups* (Yahoo!, 2008) and *Google Groups* (Google, 2009a) or on more sheltered mailing lists created specifically for language learners. Groups not intended especially for language learners, although less predictable, can provide students with a more interesting range of responses. The process of finding groups and observing how their participants discuss controversial issues can give students added insight and point them to resources they may not previously have considered.

Forming NGOs Concerned With Controversial Issues

The course has recently introduced a new element: having students form their own NGOs. This was done because after weeks of research some students were left feeling hopeless about the possibility of resolving the problems that they had identified. The first stage in the process of forming an NGO is exactly what the students in the course have just completed; it requires identification of a problem and assessment of need through original research or by synthesizing the research findings of others (Peace Corps, 2003). The next stage is to assemble ideas and resources in order to meet the identified needs or solve a defined problem in an efficient way.

Students are also given an option to create a Web site introducing their NGO or a video to promote it, which would be made available to everyone in the class as a podcast. Whichever option they choose, it is essential that they relate the research on their controversial issues and survey results to the NGO and its raison d'être. The Web site or podcast is introduced in a final presentation (for samples, see *Controversial Podcasts*, n.d.) that must also feature a skit or round-table discussion about the issue.

REFLECTIONS

Teaching this course is gratifying in that each group of students comes into it with scant knowledge of or interest in social issues, but they leave it feeling some degree of commitment to one issue and increased knowledge of others. Their stake in these issues comes from having labored arduously to separate the

Web's wheat from its chaff, deriving some kernels of truth and shaping them into something unique in the form of an NGO. Students' comments at the end of the course show that the process is a struggle, but a worthwhile one. One student commented that she gradually came to understand the point of NGOs and found making an NGO of her own to be a valuable process. Another mentioned how much he appreciated the opportunity "to be alert to controversial issues and actually 'speak out' and 'share' them," adding that he "would never have known about most of the sources [he] introduced on [his] blog otherwise."

Perhaps due to globalization and the consolidation of media outlets, students tend to gravitate toward general, global issues. Teachers may have to make special efforts to interest students in locally relevant ones. In the course described in this chapter, such issues as whaling, Japan's import ban on U.S. beef, and Japan's support of the U.S. military presence in Afghanistan have all been considered by students. However, they are almost always rejected in favor of tried-and-true topics for in-depth research such as euthanasia, cloning, the death penalty, and underage drinking. In English as a foreign language (EFL) settings, there are a number of advantages in having students research local, topical issues: (1) information is less likely to have been neatly packaged by others, requiring students to synthesize it themselves; (2) facts and opinions related to the issue are likely to be more plentiful in the students' first language, decreasing the temptation to plagiarize; and (3) there is more potential for teachers to learn from students, creating a genuine context for communication.

The use of videos and podcasts is new to the course. However, these seem to be a natural progression due to the increased exploitation of podcasts and *YouTube* (YouTube, 2008) videos by the controversial issue groups in the course of their research. Every recent group has embedded *YouTube* videos related to their topic in their blogs. This greater use of multimedia sources, as well as students' original podcasts, provides rich opportunities for students to improve their listening comprehension, an aspect of the course that previous groups felt had been lacking. Because exposure to the target language in EFL settings is particularly problematic, this has been one of the greatest, albeit serendipitous, changes in the course. At least one group from the last band of cohorts has continued their blogging—including embedding and commenting on relevant videos—months after the end of the semester. Although it may seem that the highly structured nature of the course might inhibit autonomy, it was found to be necessary in order to give students a secure place from which the sea of information before them could be organized and used constructively.

This chapter has described how investigating controversial issues can be used in an EFL context. In ESL situations, examining local issues can help adult students gain valuable knowledge about their adopted or host culture. Furthermore, this course, or selected parts of it (e.g., offline discussion, survey creation, blogging, brainstorming criteria for judging online content, formation of original

NGOs), would be appropriate in adult literacy programs or in vocational schools in which the codevelopment of English language, employment, citizenship, and computer skills is desirable.

Joseph V. Dias is an associate professor in the English Department of Aoyama Gakuin University, in Tokyo, Japan. His research interests include computer-assisted and task-based language learning.

APPENDIX A: WEB SITES FOR DEVELOPING CRITICAL THINKING SKILLS

Sites That Offer Guidance for Evaluating Internet Sources

- *Internet Detective* (tutorial for developing advanced Internet skills): http://www.vts.intute.ac.uk/detective/

- *Evaluating Web Sites*: http://www.lesley.edu/library/guides/research/evaluating_web.html

- *The Good, the Bad, and the Ugly or, Why It's a Good Idea to Evaluate Web Sources*: http://lib.nmsu.edu/instruction/eval.html

Sites to Test Students' Critical Analysis Skills

- *Dihydrogen Monoxide Research Division*: http://www.dhmo.org/
- *The British Stick Insect Foundation*: http://www.brookview.karoo.net/Stick_Insects/
- *Aluminum Foil Deflector Beanie*: http://zapatopi.net/afdb/
- *Feline Reactions to Bearded Men*: http://www.sree.net/web/feline.html
- *The Onion*: http://www.theonion.com/
- *Dwayne Medical Center: Male Pregnancy*: http://www.malepregnancy.com/

Additional Resources

- *Clusty* (metasearch engine that groups similar results into clusters, helping the searcher zero in on exactly what is being sought or discover unexpected relationships): http://clusty.com/

- *Blogger* (free blog-hosting site that allows users to set up nicely formatted blogs in minutes, invite others to comment on postings, and archive posts conveniently): http://www.blogger.com/

- *WordPress* (open source blog publishing system that allows more control than Blogger; files of various types can be uploaded and static pages created): http://wordpress.org/

- *SurveyMonkey* (free survey authoring and publishing service with a highly intuitive interface): http://www.surveymonkey.com/

APPENDIX B: EVALUATING THE QUALITY OF SURVEYS

Survey Topic: _____

Is there an item dealing with basic demographic data (age, gender, etc.)? yes/no

Are there any items that are . . .

misleading?	yes/no	_____
offensive?	yes/no	_____
unclear?	yes/no	_____
unanswerable?	yes/no	_____

Did this survey make you feel motivated to fill it out?   yes/no
Why or why not? _____

In the case of multiple-choice items, are any choices missing?   yes/no

Are there any spelling or grammatical errors?   yes/no
If yes, in which survey item(s)? _____

Are there a variety of (at least four) question types (e.g., multiple-choice
with one answer, multiple-choice with multiple answers,
open ended, matrix)?   yes/no

Do the question types seem suited to the kind of information
the group wants to learn from respondents?   yes/no

CHAPTER 13

Researching Pains: Iranian Students Exploring Medical English

Sue-san Ghahremani-Ghajar, Seyyed-Abdolhamid Mirhosseini,
and Hossein Fattahi

As part of a research-based English for specific purposes (ESP) course at Tehran University of Medical Sciences, in Iran, a third-term medical student named Hadi researched his mother's sciatica and discovered that her pain actually was due to a skeletal dysfunction. He explained, "We have been living with this pain for nearly ten years. . . . I hope that I can do something useful for my mother to decrease her pain."

Through his research, Hadi tried to understand the pain anew. He talked to his family and specifically to his mother, who helped him in a number of ways, including bringing out her medical history and checking her drugs. He also talked with his mother's doctors, consulted many medical texts, and struggled with readings and English medical terminology to tackle a problem that had been left almost untreated by doctors. He wrote about and discussed sciatica as well as lumbar disc herniation, degenerative disc disease, spondylolisthesis, and piriformis syndrome, among many other conditions. He went through all of these challenges only to find out that he had been misled by one word: *sciatica*. After reading a brief note in a textbook, he understood that the problem was probably not sciatica, but rather was related to the weight bearing sacroiliac joint. The risk factors present in Hadi's mother were almost the same as for sciatica. He named the dysfunction *sacrosciatica* and suggested a few simple exercises that appeared to decrease his mother's pain.

Against a backdrop of several years of critical practice in medical English education for adult language learners, this chapter presents a language discovery approach (Ghahremani-Ghajar, Mirhosseini, & Fattahi, 2007). It explores possibilities beyond mainstream conceptions of teaching ESP by suggesting how students may become involved in searching, interacting with, discovering, and owning language in real contexts.

CONTEXT

We started our challenge to transform "the institutionally ossified practices of English language education at Tehran University of Medical Sciences" (Mirhosseini, 2007, p. 108) in September 2002. With critical language education (Norton & Toohey, 2004; Pennycook, 1999) and teaching for understanding (Wiske, 1998) as our broad theoretical standpoints, we departed from the current practices of teaching medical ESP in Iran, which are based on mainstream ESP approaches that focus on register analysis (Strevens, 1977), student-centered approaches and needs analysis (Hutchinson & Waters, 1987), and, more recently, genre-based and content-based views (Bhatia, 2004; Brinton & Master, 1997; Lyster, 2007). Common underlying assumptions among these various approaches include an instrumentalist vision of language as merely a neutral means of communication, a view of language as a set of skills to be taught as separate components, and a fragmentary perspective on language and content that treats content as ancillary to language.

During the initial years, our courses included critical reading of medical and general texts; hospital observations and class dialogues about them; writing of student-research papers; and open-house presentations, panel discussions, and then workshops at the end of the term. These activities culminated in a full-year, research-based course, ESP II, for more than 120 19-year-old students who had already passed the prerequisite courses of General English and ESP I.

CURRICULUM, TASKS, MATERIALS

Initially, we pursued a research-based approach in ESP II based on current content-based approaches. However, such approaches tend to suffer from a predetermined view of content solely as a means *through* which language can be processed (Lyster, 2007). Instead, we envisaged medical content beyond a review of texts and decided to approach research by bringing students closer to real people in real-life contexts.

A real search originates from a truly felt thirst and pain. In the words of Mowlana Rumi, the great 13th century Persian poet, for the water of wisdom to spring all around, you need to look for thirst, and to be a real human being you need to experience real pain. Therefore, we started the term with students' own medical concerns. As beginning medical practitioners, our students did not know much about the medical aspects of pains, but by researching physical or psychological pains (such as stress and anxiety) of family members or friends, they became deeply involved in the course. During the two weeks following the introductory session, students were writing about their "pain" and discussing it in class dialogues.

As shown in Table 1, the students' learning journey began with class discussion of the film *Lorenzo's Oil* (Miller, 1992). Every second week, students watched part of the movie (in English), which depicts the true story of a little boy with a rare fatal disease. They took notes, raised questions, and discussed the story. Without any academic knowledge of medicine, Lorenzo's parents began researching the disease, which led them to develop a kind of oil that almost

Table 1. Language Discovery Curriculum in Medical English

Week	Research Issue
	Pain
1–3	**Searching practices** • Thinking about self, family, and society • Looking for one's most meaningful medical concerns • Writing and e-mailing weekly accounts of the pain
	Classroom practices • Reading brief texts about medical research • Engaging in whole-class discussions about the research of pain • Engaging in whole-class or small-group dialogues about an individual pain • Watching and discussing *Lorenzo's Oil* (Miller, 1992)
	Language focus • Engaging in discussions about what language learning involves • Reviewing previous experiences of learning English • Writing e-mail messages in English • Looking for English terminology related to a specific pain • Discussing mechanics of writing in students' e-mail
	People
4–6	**Searching practices** • Observing hospitals • Talking to patients, patients' families, specialists, etc. • Reviewing the new information to find a focal pain spot (specific research problem) • E-mailing weekly accounts of observations and dialogues
	Classroom practices • Reading about and discussing the act of reading • Creating brief reports about observations and dialogues • Engaging in class or group discussions about individual interactions • Watching and discussing *Lorenzo's Oil*
	Language focus • Discussing the mechanics of writing in students' e-mail • Discussing the language of students' observation reports • Holding challenging class discussions in English

Continued on p. 110

Table 1 (continued). Language Discovery Curriculum in Medical English

Week	Research Issue
	Words
7–11	**Searching practices** • Searching libraries and the Internet • Reading books and articles about the medical problem • Linking new information to the pain spot • Writing and e-mailing weekly accounts of readings
	Classroom practices • Creating brief reports about research and readings • As a whole class, sharing texts found by individual students • Engaging in class or group discussions about individual readings • Watching and discussing *Lorenzo's Oil*
	Language focus • Commenting on students' e-mail • Discussing aspects of reading medical texts • Raising the issue of reading between the lines • Reporting students' types of language discoveries • Holding challenging class discussions in English
	Integration
12–14	**Searching practices** • Reviewing and integrating information • Creating a meaningful picture of the particular pain spot • Providing suggestions or questions for further exploration • Writing and e-mailing progress reports
	Classroom practices • Integrating information in class or group discussions • Commenting on individual students' research
	Language focus • Discussing individual students' research in English • Writing longer integrated research reports • Applying language discoveries in students' writing • Challenging the language of students' writing
	Presentation
15–16	**Searching practices** • Reviewing possible forms of presenting research • Deciding on a suitable presentation format • Presenting research process and learnings • Asking for teacher's comments via e-mail
	Classroom practices • Discussing suitable forms of presenting pain and research for individual students • Discussing presentation forms (workshop, panel, etc.)
	Language focus • Writing a final reflective report on the entire research process • Orally presenting the research to a large audience

stopped the progress of the disease. This impressive story was an example of the type of real search that the students could undertake.

Throughout the term, the teacher reviewed students' weekly e-mail messages about their research and made notes about issues relating to the research process as well as different aspects of their written language. The class discussions usually started with the teacher's comments about these issues and suggestions about critical reading, dealing with medical terminology, structural aspects of writing, general organization of writing, and the writer's position. The rest of class time was mainly spent on student discussions about these general issues or in dealing with individual students' research points.

Academic research usually needs to go a long way before it can improve the lives of patients in the context of their daily lives. In class discussions, we debated how medical research could become more relevant to real people. To embody these debates in their search, students focused on people who could, in one way or another, contribute to their understanding of the pain. As students broke from the confinements of lectures and textbooks, they found an abundance of sources. Student writing during Weeks 4–6 showed that these sources could be a patient, a patient's relative, a doctor, a classmate, or a university professor, among many others.

"Words" were the focus of the next 5 weeks of the course as students consulted a wide variety of medical textual resources, including reference books and journal articles as well as their university textbooks, and searched the Internet. They summarized and annotated the sources and tried to integrate the information they found with the information gathered from their interactions with people in order to make meaningful inferences about the pain that they were researching.

The diverse and contextual nature of the students' reading would not have been possible in another approach to teaching this course. Learning medical English became part of a broader context of meaningful learning. Students acquired language as a means of learning how to help the people who were important to them.

Toward the end of the term, students reviewed and integrated different aspects of their research to gain a more holistic and meaningful picture of the particular pain being researched. They continued to write and e-mail progress reports and to discuss their challenges in group discussions or whole-class tasks. They also developed more comprehensive research reports.

During the last 2 weeks of the term, students explored possible forms of presentation to determine the format that they believed could best present their research process and discoveries. To wrap up the term, they wrote a learning journey report that reflected on their chosen pain as well as their discoveries, learning, and challenges throughout the term. Finally, in a special conference-style event, they presented their research to a large audience of students and teachers.

Through writing e-mail; discussing pains; finding, observing, and talking to people; reading and writing about words; watching and discussing *Lorenzo's*

Oil (Miller, 1992); and sharing in class discussions, students focused on various formal aspects of the language of their search. Their language discoveries included insights into academic and nonacademic language, spoken and written discourse, and making critical inferences. Their discoveries also included words, expressions, and grammatical structures. One such instance of critical inferences appeared while discussing an early scene of the movie, in which Lorenzo is restless at school. The students focused on the word *hyperactive,* which the school principal uses to describe Lorenzo. Students discussed the lexical components of the word as well as the negative labeling that irritated Lorenzo's mother.

These language learning experiences are characterized by three major features that distinguish them from mainstream language learning. First, the linguistic microelements are learned in a natural context of medical English through personally meaningful struggles with content rather than as decontextualized static language samples. Second, the language points that are learned are multilayered and may help students become involved with language in its full capacity rather than at mere semantic or pragmatic word and structure levels. Finally, language and its components are discovered in an authentic context by learners rather than spoon-fed to them through lectures.

REFLECTIONS

The research practices illustrated in this chapter are based on a view of language as a practice that creates people's understanding, a view of learning as a restless struggle and a commitment to gaining internal and external strength, and a view of research as honest "searching for truth or seeking answers to burning questions and passions" (Fasheh, 2003, ¶ 5). This lived experience creates transformative possibilities, inspiration, and hope for language learning in medical contexts and possibly for other language education contexts. It also may provide possibilities for questioning current assumptions regarding language education and for pursuing learning opportunities on the basis of a transformed view of English language education in content areas.

Researching pain resonates with each of us. For Ghahremani-Ghajar, the medical students taking ESP courses back in the 1980s were encountering pains that were too obvious to ignore. Their lives were so deeply rooted in their community that there was little need for reminding them of their pain. Therefore, they readily viewed foreign language learning as part of their responsibility to do something about the pain that the whole community shared. However, in recent years, the lives of students seem to be detached from their surroundings because they have been taken in by the prestige of academia and modern life. Nonetheless, the research that these young students pursued in our course gives us hope for more meaningfully situating academic practices in community life.

Through his learning journey with his students, Mirhosseini realized that research could become more personally relevant and contextualized for students when they do not rely totally on textual knowledge. Perhaps only a few students' research would qualify as methodical academic research, but the pain, people, words, and texts were quite meaningful to them. As a medical doctor, Fattahi reflected that he felt safer and stronger with a community of medical students working sincerely on the pain of real people.

However, in transforming practices by using the language discovery approach to teaching medical English, there will be a number of major challenges. First, student expectations and preconceptions about language learning as a neatly delineated process of absorbing the knowledge of vocabulary, grammar, and communication often make them resistant to participation in demanding and apparently disorganized research. Second, after years of schooling with teacher-initiated activities, students often lack self-initiative and recoil from uncertainty. Finally, students worry that a radically different approach to language learning may not prepare them for the English subsection of the National Comprehensive Examination of Basic Sciences for medical students, which consists largely of multiple-choice test items on terminology and grammar.

Despite these challenges, facilitating language discovery rather than merely teaching a foreign language, coupled with the process of researching a particular pain rather than researching a general academic interest, can create meaningful language learning practices. The specific practical procedures presented here will need to be modified for other contexts, but such a research-based discovery approach could be introduced into many ESP and English for academic purposes courses in content areas such as engineering, social sciences, professional training, and nursing, as well as into general content-based learning for intermediate- and advanced-level language learners. By engaging in such practices, learners may authentically explore and experience language while integrating information and presenting their work. The fundamental requirement of the realization of a language discovery approach is an understanding of language as a complex sociocontextual practice and learning as a challenging process of discovery.

ACKNOWLEDGMENTS

We would like to thank our community of friends and colleagues who have been with us throughout the past 5 years of exploring medical English at Tehran University of Medical Sciences: Hossein Mohammadi Doostdar, Azin Rahimi, Ali Sedighi Gilani, Abolghasem Jazayeri, Mehdi Mollaei, Soudeh Oladi, Fahimeh Gholamhossein, Arezou Kashani, Farinoush Ebrahimi, Marjan Chinianpour, Shiva Bakhtiari, Hossein Sattari, Ehsan Sattarian, Masoumeh Ghomi, Samaneh Oladi, Parvaneh Hosseini, Mahnaz Feiz, Golriz Mirshahvelayati, Saeideh Karimi, Mahsa Sheikhan, and Mahtab Janfada. We are also grateful to all of our students, whose brilliant ideas and meaningful challenges created invaluable learning experiences during our learning journeys with them.

Sue-san Ghahremani-Ghajar explored second language education in her PhD studies at the University of Ottawa. She continues her explorations in language education as a faculty member at Al-Zahra University, in Tehran, Iran. Her work has appeared in Language, Culture and Curriculum; ITL: Review of Applied Linguistics; *and* Al-Zahra University Journal of Humanities.

Seyyed-Abdolhamid Mirhosseini is relearning his academic studies (an MA in TEFL from the University of Tehran) with his primary, secondary, and postsecondary students in Iran. His papers have appeared in venues including Applied Linguistics *and* Language, Culture and Curriculum, *and his book reviews in such journals as* Language in Society *and* Discourse & Society.

Hossein Fattahi began his career as a medical doctor, having studied at Shaheed Beheshti University of Medical Sciences, in Tehran, Iran. Questioning mainstream academic approaches to health and illness led to his explorations of medical discourse. His current challenges include understanding the language context of medical education and medicine.

Innovations
Within a Course

CHAPTER 14

Field Trips With Japanese Student Ethnographers

Gregory Strong

A field trip to the city's largest cathedral, a tour of a synagogue led by its rabbi, or an invitation to prayer at a mosque downtown all offer rich opportunities for learning English through exploring different cultures. These visits represent only a few of many potential project-based tasks incorporating ethnographic interviews, site-based description, and participant observation. After the field trip, small groups of students can share their discoveries in class and write reflective comments about different cultural values. This type of project also helps students understand how cultural values may affect intercultural communication.

CONTEXT

Field trips remain a well-established component of English as a second language (ESL) courses. An early advocate, Wissot (1970) argues that they can serve as a means of extending language learning into realistic settings and promoting greater cultural awareness. More recent supporters include Buchanan (1992), who described a topic-based ESL curriculum with field trips to an electronics factory, a planetarium, and a museum. After participating in these activities, students reflected on their feelings as observers and participants. Diaz, Justicia, and Levine (2002) reported on an intensive language program at a community college that combined field trips with vocabulary workshops, role-play, and speech practice. However, important distinctions exist between the use of field trips in the past and a current ethnographic approach in which students generate their own questions and record the data.

In addition, incorporating field trips into English as a foreign language (EFL) curricula is comparatively new, in part due to prevailing conceptions of language teaching. Roberts, Byram, Barro, Jordan, and Street (2001) contend that the goal of communicative language teaching should be reinterpreted to include understanding another culture as well as acquiring language because understanding another culture would enable a language learner to achieve the larger goal of intercultural communicative competence. Their observations have been largely derived from curriculum development projects in the modern languages departments of many British universities. These projects are designed to prepare students for a year of study abroad, an increasingly popular option among undergraduates. One of these projects is an ethnographic research project at Thames Valley University, which begins with 45 hours of instruction in culture and ethnography in students' sophomore year. This is followed by study abroad, during which the students carry out an ethnographic study. After they return to Britain, they write a 7,000-word ethnographic report.

At present, there are few published accounts of ethnographic tasks developed for language students to study culture. Among them is the Language and Residence Abroad (LARA) Project at Oxford Brookes University, in England, which includes a unit on cultural attitudes toward food, in which students ask friends and acquaintances about such things as the parts of animals that they consider edible and the vegetables that they prefer. Afterward, students write about their findings. Another is described by Murray and Bollinger (2001), who had small groups of Japanese university students exchange e-mail with pen pals in other countries, question guest speakers who were invited to class, interview other students who had been abroad, and report about their experiences on video. They note that with the help of question sheets the interviews could be undertaken with students of low language ability. In one of the few studies of the application of ethnographic techniques to language and cultural learning, Robinson-Stuart and Nocon (1996) trained elementary-level Spanish speakers to conduct ethnographic interviews for a cross-cultural project in a university-level Spanish course. The researchers reported that the project improved the students' attitudes toward studying Spanish and helped them better understand their own culture. They concluded that the project work also assisted students in viewing another culture from an *emic* or insider perspective instead of the *etic* view, the traditional study of a culture through externals: "food, festivals, buildings, and other cultural institutions" (p. 434).

Some educators might argue that to label classroom tasks as "ethnography" misuses the term. Students lack the theoretical training and experience to design and conduct genuine ethnographic field research. However, others describe the benefits of teaching language through introducing ethnographic research. McCurdy, Spradley, and Shandy (2005), employ this approach with their undergraduate ethnography students as "a *discovery* process rather than a *theory-driven* process" (p. viii).

A discovery process that introduces ethnographic techniques with language and culture learning is an apt description of the field trip project in the language classroom. Moreover, the process enables students to make their own discoveries about culture. The field trip project described here was part of a lecture course in the English department at Aoyama Gakuin University, in Tokyo, Japan, for some

50 students studying intercultural communication. With the exception of several exchange students from Asia and North America, the students were Japanese and had an upper-intermediate level of English language ability. All were in their third or fourth year of studies. Many of the Japanese students had studied abroad in 3- to 4-week summer language programs, and a few had studied abroad for part of their elementary or high school education. For these reasons, class interest in intercultural communication was high.

CURRICULUM, TASKS, MATERIALS

Preparing for the Field Trip

A central tenet of intercultural communication is that it is influenced by social and cultural values. Samovar and Porter (2000) argue that the most important of these is "a culture's orientation toward such things as God, nature, life, death, the universe, and other philosophical issues that are concerned with the meaning of life and with 'being'" (p. 11). Ting-Toomey and Chung (2005) add that to understand a culture one must analyze "the deep level culture" (p. 33), the fundamental beliefs underlying it. To examine this level of culture, I developed a field trip project consisting of visits to religious institutions in Tokyo. Because most of the students in the class were Japanese who would be familiar with Shinto and Buddhist temples, I arranged to visit other religious centers. A section the class went to a synagogue, while the remainder of the class went to either a Catholic cathedral or a mosque. If a student was familiar with the religion or the place of worship, he or she was assigned to a different group. Preparation for the visit included consulting Web sites and reading articles from intercultural communication textbooks that described the development of Judaism, Christianity, and Islam and their central beliefs.

Following Roberts et al. (2001), who suggest that studying another culture begins with a study of one's own, I included readings and discussion on religious observances in Japan. This study surprised the class because so few of the students attend regular religious services that they generally believed that they were not religious. However, Shinto and Buddhist rites and visits to shrines form an important part of modern Japanese cultural life. A new prime minister will visit the ancient Shinto shrine at Ise, associated with Amaterasu, the sun goddess, and offer prayers on forming a new government cabinet. Also, Japanese people often marry with Shinto wedding rites and are buried with a Buddhist funeral. Many Japanese pray at shrines and temples on the first few days of the New Year, *Hatsumode,* or on other auspicious occasions such as before taking school entrance exams. In addition, certain mountains have Shinto shrines; the most famous, Mount Fuji, serves as a national symbol. Through readings and discussions, the students began to realize that religious beliefs and practices underpin many aspects of Japanese culture and might therefore become a factor in cross-cultural communication.

Other class activities involved small-group discussions, responding to reading comprehension questions, and making comparisons between Buddhism, Judaism, Christianity, and Islam. Students completed charts comparing such aspects as the central beliefs, historical and geographical origins, and sacred texts of these religions. Where possible, personal interviews and clips from documentaries about each of these religions provided note-taking and listening opportunities in class.

Field Trips and the Ethnographic Report

To prepare for the field trips, I contacted a synagogue, a cathedral, and a mosque and asked for an English-speaking guide at each who would serve as a "cultural informant" to conduct a tour. Also it was important to get permission to photograph and sketch the interiors of these buildings as part of the site-based description aspect of the project. Before the visit, students were divided into small groups in which they prepared descriptive questions for their cultural informant and practiced asking them through role-plays. These questions were adapted from Spradley (1979), whose primer, *The Ethnographic Interview*, remains a valuable reference today. The four descriptive question types in Figure 1 generate other questions, in this case, using modals such as *could, should,* and *would*, a language feature that could be pointed out to students. These questions, in turn, elicit further details.

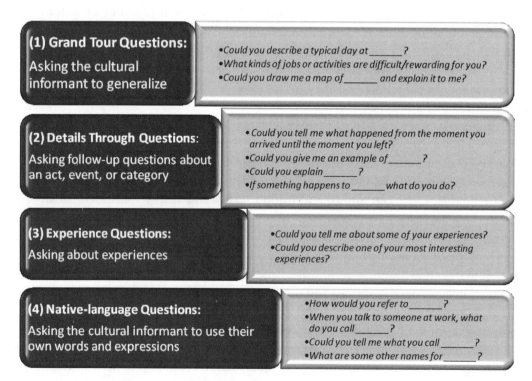

(1) Grand Tour Questions:
Asking the cultural informant to generalize

- Could you describe a typical day at _____ ?
- What kinds of jobs or activities are difficult/rewarding for you?
- Could you draw me a map of _____ and explain it to me?

(2) Details Through Questions:
Asking follow-up questions about an act, event, or category

- Could you tell me what happened from the moment you arrived until the moment you left?
- Could you give me an example of _____ ?
- Could you explain _____ ?
- If something happens to _____ what do you do?

(3) Experience Questions:
Asking about experiences

- Could you tell me about some of your experiences?
- Could you describe one of your most interesting experiences?

(4) Native-language Questions:
Asking the cultural informant to use their own words and expressions

- How would you refer to _____ ?
- When you talk to someone at work, what do you call _____ ?
- Could you tell me what you call _____ ?
- What are some other names for _____ ?

Figure 1. Four Descriptive Question Types for an Ethnographic Report (adapted from Spradley, 1979, pp. 86–91)

To replicate the documentation of ethnographic research and to facilitate student discussion and self-reflections after the visit, each group used their notes to complete a report that was divided into five sections. Section 1 consisted of a short primer on the history of Judaism, Christianity, or Islam in Japan. Student explanations had to use appropriate academic form and incorporate quotations and other information taken from pamphlets during the visit or from Web sites viewed beforehand as preparation. Section 2 was a transcription of a recording of the group's questions and the cultural informant's answers during the visit. In Section 3, students prepared a taxonomy or "domain" of the activities provided by a cathedral; then they listed categories such as the Holy Mass and the Administration of the Archdiocese and subcategories such as liturgical rites and the archives of the archdiocese (see Appendix A). For Section 4, students created a schematic diagram of the layout of the synagogue, church, or mosque with labeled photographs of objects and different parts of the site (see Appendix B). Section 5 comprised the notes made after a follow-up visit as a participant observer of a religious service.

Research Exchange

After their field trip, each group prepared a written report. As Mohan (1986) has pointed out, key visuals such as the taxonomy or the diagram provide excellent scaffolding for writing as well as discussions. A taxonomy with categories and subcategories assists students in making classifications, comparisons, and contrasts and in choosing the appropriate transitions with words such as *some* and *many* and phrases like *for example* and *compared to*. A diagram suggests the use of comparative terms and certain prepositions. Some class time was provided for assembling this final report because of the difficulty of four or five students being able to meet at the same time outside of class hours. Copies were made after class so that each group member could prepare for a research exchange in the following class.

In the next class, these reports were shared in groups of three, with a student from each field trip in each trio. Finally, the students wrote self-reflections on their group's research and explanations, and on the presentations that they had heard from other groups, addressing such questions as the following: How would you compare religion in Japan to what you have heard? What was the most interesting thing your group discovered? How did the visit change some of your ideas? Then students returned to their original groups to discuss their observations, and I collected their written self-reflections along with the reports for assessment.

In course evaluations, students were overwhelmingly positive about the field trips, saying that they had learned something about other cultures without leaving Japan. Comments included "It was a precious chance for me to touch other cultures," "I never knew these groups were in Tokyo," and "I felt as if I were in a foreign country." The students compared the course quite favorably with others that consisted solely of conventional lectures and note taking.

REFLECTIONS

Places of worship, such as a synagogue, a church, and a mosque, are repositories of a deep level of culture. The Japanese students visiting these places were
exposed to cultural belief systems very different from their own. As rich an opportunity as this project-based task can be, with some students, or in some countries,
and in certain contexts, such visits might be too controversial or simply unsuitable
for the curricular objectives.

Needless to say, numerous other field trips are possible in an EFL setting and
can employ a similar methodology if the students have at least an intermediate
level of language ability. Our other field trips have included visiting the annual
fair at an international school, attending a theater when there was a performance
in English, and touring the production plant of an English-language newspaper.
At the school fair, some students did projects involving comparative education,
learning about the school curriculum, interviewing people at the fair, taking
photographs, and studying the premises. Others compared the foods available at
the fair, looked at the cultural aspects of children's games, or participated in other
activities. The English theater performance field trip began with teaching part of
the script and included learning about directing, acting, and creating stage light-
ing and sound cues. In the newspaper visit, students learned about newspaper
production, offset printing, and how satellite transmissions and digital photog-
raphy are used. This field trip also provided students with insights into careers in
journalism and marketing.

A similar approach could be taken with visits to foreign businesses or manu-
facturing plants in which a tour could be provided in English. These field trips
are possible in the major cities of many non-English-speaking countries. Other
opportunities might include visits to embassy libraries, the offices of nongovernmental organizations, or international trade shows or educational conferences
where students might serve as volunteers in exchange for free admission to the
lectures and book fair. Most of these organizations welcome the opportunity for
community outreach.

Of course, in an ESL environment, there are many more possibilities for field
trips, including traditional visits to museums and art galleries as well as to such
places as hospitals, fire stations, city council rooms, courthouses when trials are
in session, or even combining a field trip with a university campus orientation.
Altogether, these visits offer students potential insights into a community and
provide language learning practice.

Field trips offer language students the chance to see English in environments
outside the classroom. For students in largely monocultural contexts like Japan,
the existence of these institutions, indeed of English language communities, often
comes as a surprise. Most EFL teachers will find that their students have had little
experience with this active learning style and that introducing them to it requires

careful explanation and student preparation. However, no classroom activities or materials can replicate the excitement of seeing the target language in use. Furthermore, field trips offer students the chance to use English in a meaningful way by interacting with native speakers who are not their teachers.

Gregory Strong is an English professor and program coordinator at Aoyama Gakuin University, in Tokyo, Japan. He has also worked in China and Canada as a teacher educator and curriculum designer. He has contributed to various TESOL books and has published fiction and the biography Flying Colours: The Toni Onley Story *(Harbour Press, 2002).*

APPENDIX A: SAMPLE TAXONOMY FOR A FIELD TRIP TO A CATHEDRAL

Function	Services Offered	Additional Details
Celebration of the holy Mass	• Prayers to the congregation • Priest gives a homily (a reading and interpretation of the gospel) • Baptisms	• Japanese Mass for Catholics • Korean Mass for Catholics
Celebration of other holy sacraments	• Weddings • Funerals • Hearing confessions	• The times for weddings and funerals reserved in advance • Confession offered at various times during the day
Administration of the Archdiocese	• Liaison with Catholic International offices • Chancery office • Archives of the archdiocese	• Administrative center for 75 churches providing religious services in Japanese, English, Tagalog, Spanish, and other languages • Also two seminaries, six universities, eight junior colleges, 14 high schools, 13 middle schools, 95,362 Catholics
Caritas No Le House of Caritas Welfare Center	• Outreach programs with mandate to help those in need • Aishin kindergarten	• Consultation with the municipality to identify the needy such as homeless people, those with mental or physical disabilities, and a mission to the hearing impaired • Programs to provide daycare for young mothers

International Youth Association	• Catholic youth group offers recreation and service opportunities, building leadership, and contributing to disaster relief • Shinsei Kaikan Student Center	
Residence	• Archbishop's residence, and retirement home for aged priests	
National programs	• Peace Week, August observance of WWII's end • Promote awareness of 26 Japanese saints martyred in Nagasaki in 1597 • Promote awareness of 188 beatified Japanese martyrs	• Commemorative 24-hour period of prayer at the cathedral • Sponsors public lectures on Article 9, the "No War" clause of the Japanese postwar constitution • Memorial walk in the archdiocese

APPENDIX B: PARTIAL LAYOUT OF A TOKYO MOSQUE

Exterior View

Dome and Lattice Fence

 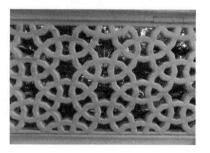

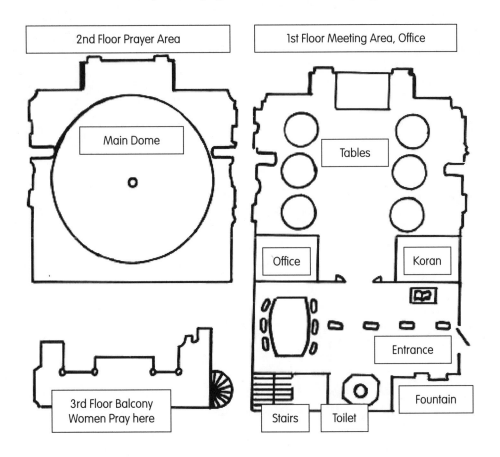

2nd Floor Prayer Area

1st Floor Meeting Area, Office

Main Dome

Tables

Office

Koran

Entrance

3rd Floor Balcony
Women Pray here

Fountain

Stairs

Toilet

CHAPTER 15

Role-Playing With Fire: Hot Topics and Heated Discussions

Christopher Stillwell

An important way of limiting the damage caused by forest fire is to intentionally and strategically set a few small fires in advance, creating buffers to help bring it under control. In a similar fashion, a language teacher may use role-play as a way to engage in controlled explorations of hot topics in order to establish acceptable ways of dealing with such material. Even the tamest of classroom discussions can unexpectedly end up in sensitive territory, challenging students' values and potentially "outing" privately held beliefs and behaviors. This can be a particularly important concern for teachers of adult language learners because their needs for self-direction and the use of relevant, practical, and even experiential material can often lead to explorations of real-life issues.

When used responsibly, hot topics can motivate engagement in class activity, but those who play carelessly will surely get burned. This chapter provides suggestions for establishing an appropriate environment for the safe use of role-play, creating powerful learning opportunities where language is used not merely for its own sake but rather for the purpose of sharing and understanding differing points of view.

CONTEXT

The work discussed in this chapter was first inspired by my exposure to hot topics as educationally valuable content in seminars at the International Center for Cooperation and Conflict Resolution at Columbia University. I developed related material for an English as a second language (ESL) course at Cambridge Schools, an intensive English program for adult language learners in New York City. The class participants were primarily Japanese students in their 20s who were at the upper-intermediate to advanced level. They were continuing their studies in small

5-week elective courses that were tailored to their interests in building vocabulary and enhancing listening and speaking abilities. Conflict-related topics were selected to engage the students in language use that went beyond rote practice, which challenged them to use their skills to better share and understand differing points of view.

CURRICULUM, TASKS, MATERIALS

In most communicative language teaching situations, the use of controversy will stimulate conversation and engage learners. To help students process their reactions and grow through their exposure to such material, they should record their reflections in journals. Such activity can also prove valuable for developing writing fluency and scaffolding deep and meaningful discussion during debriefing sessions.

To nurture an environment where students feel comfortable participating, the promotion of acceptance in the group is critical. Dörnyei and Murphey's (2003) *Group Dynamics in the Language Classroom* provides many useful insights, including the suggestion that getting students to learn the names of their classmates can play an important part in group bonding. On a day-to-day basis, making sure that students regularly mix into different groups can further enhance class participation as students with different backgrounds and language abilities work together. For example, an early role-play might involve small groups of students preparing for and then acting out visits to a talk show, in which one student plays the host while others play the guests.

Getting Started

Students may feel uncomfortable with "acting" at first, so early role-plays should be done without observers so as to reduce self-consciousness about performing. Using only two-person scenarios at first is also advisable so that there is less potential for shy students to rely on others to fill in the silences. Ladousse (1987) notes that care should be taken to make sure the language requirements of the role-play are not beyond the learners' abilities; otherwise the learners may end up undermining the language goals by switching to their native tongue.

It is probably best to begin with topics that will not absorb students in heated debates about closely held beliefs. With completely fictional situations, students can begin developing the skills to effectively express (and truly listen to) differing opinions. For the diverse classroom, such situations may involve disputes related to everyday relationship issues, difficulties ensuing from borrowed items returned in imperfect condition, and trouble collaborating on a group project. For instance, students can act out a simple situation like the one detailed in Figure 1.

Public Information

Roles: Partners A and B, coworkers/classmates

Scenario: The boss/teacher has assigned you a partner to work with on a major project. You are supposed to work together on a moderately lengthy report (20 pages or so) and a 10-minute presentation, but you are having trouble working together.

Objective: Resolve the tension and establish a satisfying working relationship.

Special Information for Partner A Only
- Whenever you try to schedule a meeting, your partner says that he or she is too busy.
- Whenever you do work together, your partner seems unprepared.
- You feel that you are doing most of the work, and that your partner is taking advantage of you.

Special Information for Partner B Only
- You are doing everything you can to contribute to this project, but no matter what you do, your partner seems unsatisfied.
- Last week, when you met, you found that your partner had already done a part of the work that was supposed to be your job (but he or she never said anything to you about taking that part of the work).
- Whenever you talk about schedules, your partner quickly gets irritated by your busy calendar. Does he or she want you to give up your other responsibilities just so you can do this project?

Figure 1. Dispute on a Group Project

Scaffolding the Interaction

All students should receive copies of their role cards for Public Information, which can be openly discussed as a class. The teacher can lead a brainstorming session to generate a list of vocabulary words that could prove useful in the role-play, including informal or colloquial ways of expressing disagreement and frustration. To preserve the spontaneous nature of the role-play and to ensure that the students will actually listen and respond to one another, the teacher needs to make sure that this preparation remains at the level of jotting down notes, not writing scripts. Finally, all Partner As should be given the Special Information for Partner A Only to look over together, brainstorming specific approaches and things to say. Meanwhile the Partner Bs do the same with their special information.

Before the As pair up with Bs and begin the role-play, the teacher should confirm that the instructions and scenario are absolutely clear, perhaps by eliciting responses from students about what they are now expected to do. For students who tend to finish activities with dubious efficiency, it may be useful to assert that they are responsible for keeping their conversation going. However, the teacher should have an additional activity for those who finish early. Also, while the teacher still has the students' attention, the procedure for ending the role-plays should be established. For instance, the teacher may set an alarm to go off when the time is up or decide on another obvious signal, such as turning off the light or raising a hand.

Action and Reaction

While the students are engaged in their role-play, the teacher should unobtrusively observe their interactions. The teacher also should take note of the interesting choices that students make as well as language-related points (both good and bad) that come up. These observations can be shared in the end as a part of whole-class discussion and debriefing. Finally, for the sake of ensuring lively discussion during the debriefing, it is best to cut off a role-play before interest in the topic has been exhausted (Davis, 1993).

Once the role-play has been cut off, students should have a chance to reflect on and discuss their work. To allow for maximum language practice and to scaffold a whole-class discussion, the students should be given a few minutes to write reflections in their journals. This should be followed by time to debrief with their partners prior to sharing with the whole group. Specific questions such as the following can guide these conversations: Which parts went particularly well? Which parts did not? What made you feel uncomfortable as you expressed disagreement? What might you do differently in the future?

El-Shamy (2005) suggests that having students change locations can be an effective way of mentally and physically bringing everyone into a different space for the whole-class discussion and debriefing. Sitting in a big circle has the added benefit of breaking the pairs up and focusing attention on the group. Teachers may be tempted to trim or cut this discussion when the schedule becomes cramped, but El-Shamy notes that it is a mistake to do so because this debriefing is essential to establishing and reinforcing what has been learned. These are her suggested questions: "What happened?", "How do you feel?", "What did you learn?", "How will you apply what you learned?" (p. 61). In the end, the teacher should wrap things up with a summary of what has been accomplished.

Variations

Role-plays typically require a fair bit of time for students to become familiar with the scenario. It can be wise to make use of this time investment to attempt more than one version in class. There are a number of ways in which a second attempt at a role-play can yield deeper learning, including these:

- *Give it a twist:* Make the second attempt different. The teacher can do this, for example, by giving the partners important new information about their parts or making restrictions or recommendations on the type of language to be used. Another method is to get students to change partners in order to listen and respond to differences in the tactics and language used.

- *Engage in academic controversy:* For role-plays related to serious issues, students can first prepare and act a role related to one side of the issue, then switch parts and try again. When debriefing after the second attempt, students can aim to synthesize both points of view in a way that satisfies all parties (Johnson & Johnson, 1995). This can be an effective way to help them go beyond simple right-or-wrong assessments of issues. They can learn to appreciate others' viewpoints, seeing that there is always more than one side to an issue.

REFLECTIONS

A useful reading on the topic of cultural sensitivity is Avruch's (2002) "What Do I Need to Know About Culture?" It warns against seeing culture as prescriptive (e.g., "He's from Japan, so he's more interested in the collective than the individual"), expecting members of a culture to be representatives (e.g., "You're Mexican. How do Mexicans feel about this immigration law?"), and stereotyping. For the latter, Avruch suggests a simple but effective exercise to bring "All" statements (e.g., "All Chinese are hard workers") back down to earth: In place of the culture in question, substitute your own identity (e.g., American, Canadian), and see how accurate it feels ("All _____ are hard workers").

It is also important to remember that many tricky issues could best be labeled intractable or unresolvable. For instance, Lewicki, Saunders, and Minton (2001) note that stances on debates related to the Arab-Israeli conflict are often framed by religious beliefs. Surely, the same issue applies to stances in other debates, such as abortion, gay marriage, and sex education. Trained mediators face daunting challenges trying to frame issues differently and seek common ground. Therefore, for the adult language learner, it can be important to keep a realistic perspective on such issues, being prepared to agree to disagree (at best) and avoiding unrealistic expectations for satisfying closure to such discussions. Topics such as these require a delicate hand to keep the heat of discussion from turning destructively inflammatory.

Christopher Stillwell has taught EFL/ESL learners in Spain, the United States, and Japan for 16 years as well as TESOL graduate students at Teachers College, Columbia University. Currently a lecturer at Kanda University of International Studies, in Chiba, Japan, his interests include using conflict resolution techniques to facilitate learning.

CHAPTER 16

A Case for Discussion

Ann F. V. Smith

Case-based teaching is popular in many university faculties, including business, medicine, and law, because case studies introduce simulations of real-life situations. Thus case analysis, which draws on the knowledge and past experience of participants, provides a fitting forum for seminar discussion and the development of genuine negotiation, group collaboration, and critical awareness.

Case studies are particularly appropriate for developing communicative competence with adult language learners in English for academic purposes (EAP). This chapter explores the use of cases to develop discussion skills in the Oral Communication and Study module of the University of Nottingham's undergraduate Foundation Certificate. A case example integrating global issues content illustrates the teaching process, and the chapter closes with a reflection on some of the challenges involved.

CONTEXT

The Foundation Certificate began at the University of Nottingham's U.K. campus in 2006 and enrols an international multilingual cohort of young adult students. Their experience with English-speaking cultures and their entry levels vary widely, from low-intermediate to almost native speaker. The students aim to gain a 70% grade average across all of their modules because this is what is required to enter an undergraduate degree program in the University of Nottingham's School of Business.

This programme aims to equip students for the expectations of a higher education degree by providing 50% EAP and study skills and 50% introductory content courses. The two 30-credit EAP modules integrate students' language knowledge with global issues content. Cases are a key module component in the second semester of Oral Communication and Study and are integrated into the assessment through a case project presentation and an observed group discussion. This format also applies to the Foundation Programme at the University of Nottingham's Ningbo, China, campus, which began in 2004.

Case-based teaching is used to develop seminar discussion skills that encourage group collaboration and teamwork through the sharing of experience, perspectives, and alternatives. Students must listen actively, elicit and question others, and clarify and justify opinions on the spot, all of which promotes fluency and appropriacy and helps students overcome nervousness.

To develop these skills, "instruction needs to ensure that learners develop both a rich repertoire of formulaic expressions and a rule based competency" following R. Ellis's (2005a, p. 3) first principle of instructed language acquisition. Functional language, or speech acts, is popular in EAP and useful in case discussions because it provides students with conversational routines to engage, agree, speculate, or evaluate. Examples can be found in many course books and supplementary texts, and components of spoken grammar (e.g., sentence heads, tails, tag questions) can be added. Rodgers (2001) explains the ongoing popularity of the approach: "Now new leads in discourse and genre analysis, schema theory, pragmatics, and systemic/functional grammar are rekindling an interest in functionally based approaches to language teaching" (¶ 17).

Corpus-based research has shown that native speakers also know and use a wide range of prefabricated lexical phrases or fixed phrases that can be retrieved as units. Skehan (1998) suggests that "producing speech seems to be much more a case of improvising on a clause-by-clause basis, using lexical elements (lexicalized sentence stems, or lexical phrases) wherever possible" (p. 37). Many lexical phrases, which can be checked in various spoken corpora and the Academic Word List (AWL), also have slots that can be changed to build a variety of variable expressions.

Each case study develops lexis and fluency through the discussion of typical and unusual features of a real-life contextualised event. Students draw on their experience and research, functional formulaic phrases, grammar, and cultural background to identify key issues and interact with the case in small groups (Richards, 1998). A series of questions encourages them to share, question, explore, analyse, synthesise, reflect, interpret, evaluate, speculate, and come to a consensus (Keily, 2004). Through sharing, they develop fluency and confidence and learn to respect the contradictory ideas of others. They also become more aware of their own cultural context, beliefs, and interpretations, and may even reassess their own views. Students may argue that they also pick up each other's errors, but Flowerdew (1998) and others reject this view.

The role of the teacher is not to engage in the case discussion but to act as a facilitator. During the discussion, the teacher needs to move between groups and act as a catalyst, guide, and prompter, developing critical awareness and creating links between ideas. He or she should listen actively, provide support, and ask a wide range of open-ended questions to seek opinions, extend information, focus on generalisations, or challenge opinions (Jackson, 2002).

However, developing these seminar discussion skills can be challenging. Basturkmen (2002) shows that academic discussion is generally extended and more indirect and complex than previously identified. It goes beyond the initial elicitation, informational, or directive moves because speakers frequently provide extra information, justification, or support for a point and often follow up over the course of several turns.

CURRICULUM, TASKS, MATERIALS

The module's cases incorporate controversial news stories, unusual experiences, or topics related to global issues or cross-cultural content. Most are problem-solving cases or examples of best practice that combine an authentic situation and characters to provide universal interest. They become longer and more complex as the term progresses.

Generally, students enjoy problem-based cases as they explore an open-ended controversial dilemma, identify its causes, generate and then evaluate alternative solutions, and finally make a decision or recommendation. The streetcar case in the Appendix provides an example of best practice or lessons learnt (and is used as the framework for this section of the chapter). It moves from a familiar local transportation topic and language to more general energy issues and environmentally friendly transportation alternatives. Students assess the controversial reintroduction of streetcars to the city of Nottingham and analyse why it is good practice. Following chronological order, the case, which was written by the teacher using local knowledge, describes the streetcar line development (answering who, what, why, when, where), reviews a customer evaluation, and identifies vocabulary from the AWL in bold. Open-ended discussion questions focus on particular features and encourage the exchange of opinions and perceptions.

Such a case study needs to be brief, well focused, and interesting. Begin by selecting a theme that is popular with students and then look for a local or international news item related to the theme containing a real story with real characters. The story should raise issues open to various interpretations and offer some uncertainty or difficult choices and enough detail for a full picture. Guceri and Akin (1998) suggest that the writer also consider time frame, length, level of difficulty, cultural framework, topic, tasks, and the course objectives. Of course, it can be challenging to weave all of these together into near-authentic material and ensure an appropriate level of language and structures.

In the classroom, the intersection of the case, the group discussion, and the teacher's facilitation come together through a precase phase, case analysis, and a postcase teaching process. In the precase phase, the teacher elicits (and prompts for) students' prior knowledge, language, and experience with transportation. Students then speculate on the following questions:

- Would the world be better off without cars?

- If cars were banned from cities, how would cities (e.g., Nottingham, Shanghai) change?

They give their opinions and speculate about alternative, less-polluting forms of transportation. Then they compare their language with formulaic expressions, including *definitely, likely, unlikely,* and *never,* and modal verbs for prediction and speculation. Then the teacher can encourage them to adopt the new items in the discussion.

Next, the teacher introduces the case and clearly outlines the expectations for the group discussion, explaining its focus on best practice. After reading the case introduction aloud, the teacher explains any cultural background and links to the students' own experiences. Then the teacher asks students to read the case, telling them to notice the AWL words/collocations (in bold) in context (such as *energy, innovations, initial investment, infrastructure*) and underline any time markers. Then they complete a timeline of events so that they notice time markers and tenses.

Now the teacher creates mixed groups of three to five (so that students of different nationalities and language levels collaborate) and assigns roles for the discussion, if required. During the discussion, the teacher prompts and encourages students to provide extended responses and highlight advantages, disadvantages, and functional language use. The teacher guides their focus towards features in the case that will increase critical awareness and collect language items for later consolidation activities.

In the postcase phase, groups can summarise their key points and group dynamics can be analysed. Short- or long-term and ideal or real situations can also be considered and compared to the initial predictions and speculations. In addition, language items from the case can be reviewed. Consolidation activities can link to time markers and tenses, using modals for speculation or AWL vocabulary. For homework, students investigate an alternative energy solution for transportation and prepare bullet points on a card for brief presentations.

REFLECTIONS

A case study provides a focus for a more realistic seminar-style discussion, with students engaging with the case and analysing its components. However, because many students come directly from a high school with large classes, textbooks, and a traditional chalk-and-talk-based system, some find using English discussion quite challenging. Therefore, it is essential to explain that participating in the discussions provides essential language practice, especially considering that some students are confident and more fluent while others struggle.

In addition, teachers need to help students understand that case analysis requires a combination of independent study, group involvement, and responsibility. Some students are not used to supporting their own opinions and are reluctant to question opinions in group work, preferring to work alone. Teachers should also explain that heterogeneous, multicultural groupings will develop group cohesiveness, friendship, and support as well as cross-cultural understanding.

The case method may also challenge the skills of the teacher. Occasionally, discussions are unpredictable and some students may try to dominate whilst others are shy and reluctant to participate. In addition, friendships, status, approval, power relations, and other factors can influence group dynamics. Some students may focus on the teacher and need to be encouraged to listen to student models and monitor their own errors. Others find the range of possible options uncomfortable and request the "right" answer. When providing feedback, the teacher can offer several options rather than one answer for students to consider. All students need awareness of the importance of providing encouragement and need to be provided with language samples for praising and for giving constructive reactions so that feedback and correction become shared responsibilities.

Case studies can be used in many classroom environments, including distance formats, but most teachers need to adapt or create cases tailored to meet the specific content and language needs of their students. Few previously prepared cases are appropriate for students' needs; others may be too long or too culturally specific. However, a case study can provide a catalyst for developing fluency, appropriacy, confidence, and critical awareness. The teacher can guide, facilitate, and provide functional language input during the discussion. The students, meanwhile, can explore their own underlying attitudes, beliefs, and values; elaborate on and justify their ideas; and build on the diverse opinions of others.

Ann F. V. Smith is an English for academic purposes (EAP) tutor at the Centre for English Language Education at the University of Nottingham, in England. She has extensive experience as a TESOL/EAP teacher, teacher trainer, examiner, and materials developer in Asia, Scandinavia, Canada, and the United Kingdom. Her recent publications focus on syllabus design, oral communication, and classroom practice.

APPENDIX: CASE STUDY: NECESSITY IS THE MOTHER OF INVENTION

(Vocabulary from the Academic Word List is in bold.)

Skim the case study, and then read it carefully and underline the time markers. Next, check the case details and any new vocabulary in your group, and discuss the questions at the end. Be ready to report your discussion to the class.

Introduction: The need to conserve **energy** and **seek** out **alternatives** to fossil fuel in recent years has led to **innovations** in new **energy**-efficient **transport** technologies and the production of power from a wider **range** of **sources.** In France, Britain, and China, electrified railways have speeded up travel. The Beijing-to-Shanghai 1,307-kilometer electrified line will allow trains to reach speeds of up to 300 kilometers per hour. Now, cities are looking for **innovative** ways to reduce traffic congestion as newspapers report that travel by bicycle is as fast as by car. This case study looks at the recent return of trams, or streetcars, to the city of Nottingham as an **alternative** form of **transportation**.

Nottingham has recently reintroduced trams to the city. The original horse-drawn streetcars were introduced in 1878 to replace horse-drawn buses, which had operated since 1848. In 1901, these streetcars were superseded by electrified trams and within two years there were more than a hundred trams on eight lines. By the late 1920s, some of the tram lines had been **converted** for trolley busses, which operated until the mid 1960s when the lines were removed in favour of buses.

On Monday, March 8, 2004, trams returned to the streets of Nottingham. The **initial investment** in the electrified streetcar or tram system was huge, at over £200 million. During **construction** of the first **route,** there was substantial disruption as traffic was diverted while the tracks were being laid. **Furthermore,** local businesses complained of loss of trade. Customers could not reach or park near their premises during the development of the **infrastructure.**

The streetcars offer fast, affordable travel in a comfortable, quiet **environment.** A customer satisfaction **survey** carried out in October 2004 **revealed** that passengers are generally very **positive** about the streetcar system. The **survey** showed that 96% were satisfied or very satisfied with the service offered and only 1% were dissatisfied. **Approximately** a third of passengers use the streetcar to commute to work and a quarter employ it for shopping trips. In addition, 14% make use of it to travel to school or university. Most passengers who now use the streetcar **previously** travelled by bus (63%), and less than a fifth (18%) have **transferred** from car travel (Nottingham Tram Consortium, 2005).

Light rail services have also been developed recently in cities such as Manchester (Metrolink), Newcastle (Metro), and London, where the Docklands Light Railway will transport visitors to the 2012 Olympic games sites. Light rail services, unlike streetcars, use a track that is separated from the street traffic, and in the UK most are privately owned. European cities such as Amsterdam, Oslo, and Geneva also have popular streetcar services.

Discussion Questions:

- What major transportation problems do you predict for 2020?

- Why do you think Nottingham reintroduced streetcars?

- Some people say streetcars are a waste of money. What do you think are some of the disadvantages of streetcars? Justify your suggestions with reasons.

- What would happen if supplies of petrol and diesel were restricted or ran out?

- What alternative methods can be used to generate the electricity needed for streetcars and other uses?

CHAPTER 17

Motivating Thai University Students With Radio Drama

Magdalena Kubanyiova

Ask any teacher about his or her idea of a perfect student, and the words *engaged, enthusiastic,* or *motivated* are bound to appear in the description. Although the reality of higher education English as a foreign language (EFL) contexts may not always match such an ideal, this chapter offers suggestions that can help language teachers transform the motivational dynamics of their classes. Three basic conditions that have been shown to make a difference in the quality of learners' classroom engagement are explained: autonomy-supporting teaching practice, cohesive learner groups, and stimulating tasks. To bridge the gap between theory and practice, this chapter describes a successful Radio Drama Project in an undergraduate EFL class at an international university in Thailand.

CONTEXT

This project was implemented at Assumption University, in Bangkok, with students at a lower-intermediate level who were majoring in business, management, and engineering. The majority of learners were Thai nationals, although students from countries across Asia were represented in most groups. The English department's course syllabus was literature based, with instructional materials comprising original crime short stories. These were used for a variety of purposes, including the development of intensive reading and discussion skills, essay writing, pronunciation practice, and vocabulary work, and student learning was supported through numerous additional tools, such as journals, portfolios, and extensive reading projects. The Radio Drama Project was implemented in the second half of the course, with the aim to consolidate the knowledge and skills that students had previously practised.

One of the three essential tools for enhancing learner motivation is autonomy-supporting teaching practice. Research within and outside the field of English language teaching has shown strong links between learners' perceived autonomy and their motivation to learn (Little, Ridley, & Ushioda, 2003). That is, students are intrinsically motivated to learn when they perceive themselves as being in control of their learning process, rather than when they are forced to participate in classroom tasks. Students' perception of control depends, in turn, on the extent to which they perceive their teacher as committed to their learning, and the literature has identified a number of autonomy-supporting teacher classroom behaviours that have been shown to signal such commitment. Two examples of these are providing students with informative and constructive feedback on their performance and increasing learner involvement in the learning process itself. The latter can be achieved, for example, by involving learners in the decision-making process about as many aspects of the learning process as possible, encouraging project work, or providing opportunities for self-assessment (Kubanyiova, 2004).

In addition to autonomy-supporting teacher behaviours, cohesive learner groups can increase student motivation. Two basic characteristics that set cohesive groups apart from noncohesive ones are (1) positive relationships based on high levels of acceptance and trust among the group members and (2) the pursuit of common task-related goals. Research in the area of group dynamics has found a strong link between cohesive groups and productivity. As Dörnyei and Murphey (2003) maintain, this is because individuals who care about their fellow group members feel heightened responsibility to contribute to group success and, as a result, work harder in collaboration with the others to achieve their common goal. Therefore, one of the crucial ways of increasing individual learners' motivation to participate in learning tasks seems to be a class-centred approach to teaching (Senior, 2002), which actively seeks to develop group cohesiveness. Promoting acceptance among learners is a key ingredient of such an approach, involving strategies and tasks that encourage students to learn about each other, promote various forms of interaction among group members, encourage collaboration, and provide rewarding group experiences.

Finally, students' motivation to engage in learning depends on their appraisal of the classroom tasks. Learners will find the tasks worth pursuing if they consider them meaningful, personally relevant, interesting, and attainable, but not trivial. Furthermore, for the tasks to invite meaningful student participation, their structure should allow peer interaction and learners should be able to exercise control over some aspects of the task processes or outcomes, for example, by setting their own specific short-term goals. These task characteristics enhance both collaboration and motivation.

CURRICULUM, TASKS, MATERIALS

The Radio Drama Project involves a set of interesting and challenging but not unattainable tasks. Its organisation allows students to work in collaborative teams for an extended period of time, receive informative feedback from the teacher, and exercise control over the task processes as well as the final outcome.

The implementation at Assumption University followed a multistage plan (see Figure 1) spanning approximately 5–6 weeks. The initial stages were implemented in the classroom because more guidance was required at the outset of the project, but the later stages relied on the students' working in groups in their own time outside the classroom.

The project is introduced by the teacher, who hands the students copies of the instruction sheet (see Appendix A), and they work in self-selected groups on this initial task. No more than 15–20 minutes of lesson time is required for this initial stage. In the subsequent lesson, the teacher plays a suitable sample of a radio drama with good sound effects (for excellent resources, see Palermo, 1996–2006). The main purpose is to introduce students to the key features of a radio drama and analyse the purposes of using the narrator's voice and sound effects. The possibility of creating sounds manually or downloading them from the Internet is discussed (*PacDV Free Sound Effects,* n.d.; Palermo, 1996–2006).

Students will also need to become familiar with the procedures involved in script writing. To this end, a ready-made script accompanying the sample radio drama (also found in Palermo, 1996–2006) should be analysed in class for the key features. If desired, students can get further practice by creating their own short scripts based on texts that they worked with previously in class (see Appendix B). This can either be a swift activity or it can be extended and combined with other appropriate tasks that are a regular part of the course syllabus, such as pronunciation practice (students practise stress and intonation by acting out the scripts, which will also be instrumental for the later phases of their project), grammar (turning reported speech into direct speech), or specific vocabulary work.

The task of writing a script for the actual radio drama project should be completed primarily outside the classroom, with students managing their own schedules and meetings with group members. However, if students express interest, allocate some class time to this. The teacher should ensure that students are

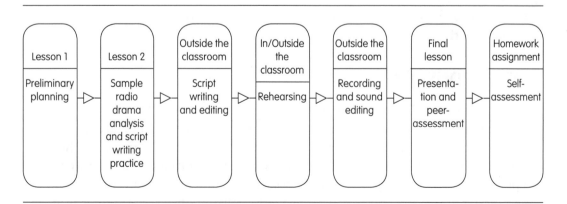

Figure 1. Implementation Stages of the Radio Drama Project

aware of the deadlines and be available for consultation when required. Detailed and prompt feedback on the groups' drafts is crucial.

Rehearsals are also done mainly in students' own time. However, the teacher should be available in case students seek assistance and to offer constructive feedback on pronunciation of individual words, stress, intonation, and natural speech. This may involve some out-of-class consultations if time constraints do not allow otherwise.

Students are now ready to record their radio dramas. Depending on availability, a variety of tools can be used, including tape recorders, computer software, or even recording studios that are often found in universities with media communication programmes. However, selecting the recording method should be the students' responsibility, and apart from providing practical suggestions when solicited, the teacher should not interfere in this stage. If sufficient support and guidance have been provided, students will be happy to take charge, often demonstrating much greater creativity, resourcefulness, and technical competence than the teacher could ever have imagined.

The final stage involves showcasing students' group projects as a way of celebrating their achievements. One way of organising this is to provide the necessary equipment, make photocopies of the scripts for the rest of the class, and let the groups present their own projects. If desired, the whole class can be involved in peer assessment. However, it is worth stressing that the main purpose of this project is to provide an opportunity in which the skills that students have acquired and practised in the course can all be put to use in a motivating way. The peer assessment in this final phase should, therefore, be focused primarily on the content of the final products and the effort the groups put into their work. In this case, all students were given blank slips of paper and asked to write encouraging comments to each group after their radio drama had been presented.

Self-assessment of the project can be done in the form of a homework assignment. In the Assumption University class, essay writing was part of the course syllabus and the aim of the writing task (see Appendix C) was twofold: to give students the chance to exercise their autonomy by evaluating their own work on the project and to have them demonstrate their essay writing skills, which were assessed by the teacher.

REFLECTIONS

The Radio Drama Project was a great success on many levels. The students' high degree of motivation was obvious from the way they managed their group work, their meticulous rewriting of scripts, the fact that they regularly sought teacher assistance, the high-quality outcome, and even their involvement in extra work. For instance, some groups submitted booklets documenting their project experience with photos, and others produced a visual version of their radio dramas in the form of a comic book, neither of which was part of the original task requirements. Some students' initially negative attitudes towards English changed quite dramatically.

It seems that it was not so much the task itself that contributed to its overall success, but rather the student participation patterns that were generated as a result of it. Working together towards a specific common goal required the groups to cooperate and gradually rely on their own resources. Furthermore, the task itself was attractive thanks to its focus. It presented an optimal challenge for students, who had to draw on a whole range of linguistic skills, including speaking, listening, writing, and pronunciation, as well as more general technology skills and organisational and managerial competencies. Scaffolding, informative feedback on interim stages of the process, and the opportunity for self-evaluation all contributed to students' perception of control over their learning, increased their responsibility, and consequently enhanced their motivation to engage fully with the task in order to secure success for the whole group. Teachers could thus design a range of tasks with similar outcomes, provided they seek ways of fostering these motivational principles.

This project lends itself to easy adoption across educational contexts because it does not place significant demands on either resources or time. With regard to resources, a tape recorder is all that is needed to make it work, and any text, including an article from a course book, a magazine article, or an extract from a graded reader, can serve as a basis for the project. In addition, depending on the teacher's objectives and the facilities available, the same procedure can be used for a number of variations, such as performing a play, making a movie, or designing a comic book (with students being the comic characters), all of which will yield similar gains. Because most of the work is done outside the classroom, the time constraints that teachers often face do not pose a serious challenge. Even those project tasks that do require class time can be easily combined with regular classroom activities. The length of the recording could also be adjusted in response to time limitations, and a short radio sketch or a dramatised 2-minute joke can produce similar outcomes within a shorter period of time.

There are, however, several points that teachers may need to consider. First, if students are not used to working in groups, some time may have to be spent on developing group work strategies prior to assigning this task. Second, in an effort to help students succeed, it may be hard for some teachers to resist the temptation to take charge of the process. However, the aim of this task is not to produce a professional drama, but to provide students with the opportunity to consolidate their knowledge in collaboration with peers, improve their attitudes towards English, and increase their motivation to continue learning when the course is over. This is unlikely to be achieved if teachers rather than students remain in control of the learning process. Finally, keeping balance between learning and fun is crucial, and a sufficient emphasis on first drafts, teacher feedback, and students' careful editing is paramount. Without such rigorous requirements, the project could easily slip into a form of entertainment with few learning gains. With these principles in mind, working with highly motivated learners need not be an unattainable ideal but a realistic aspiration of language teachers.

Magdalena Kubanyiova is a lecturer at the University of Birmingham, in England. Her interests lie in language teacher development and the social-psychological processes of language learning and teaching, especially group dynamics and motivation. She has worked with language learners and teachers in Slovakia, Thailand, and the United Kingdom.

APPENDIX A: RADIO DRAMA PROJECT
INITIAL INSTRUCTIONS

As a group, you are going to produce a radio drama (approximately 10 minutes long), which will be part of your final assessment (15%).

Topic:

(choose **ONE** of the three options)

1. Based on one of the crime stories we have read:
   a. dramatise the original short story (write a script version in your own words; however, feel free to change characters, setting, ending, etc.).
   b. continue from where the original story ends.

2. Create your own detective story.

Groups:

No more than five people in each group
ALL members must be involved in preparation stages
ALL members must be involved in performance

In today's class you will decide:

WHO: Provide a list of all members of your group, with their responsibilities; choose your group leader.

WHAT: Select the topic (which short story), and write a brief outline of either the plot or your changes to the plot (if you decided to do 1a).

WHEN: Set your timetable. Include time for script writing, script editing, rehearsals, recording (where/how are you going to do it?), and final sound editing.

At the end of the class, please submit your project proposal to the teacher. You'll need to keep in mind deadlines when designing your timetable.

APPENDIX B: SAMPLE RADIO DRAMA SCRIPT

The final scene in which Paul breaks into Rolf's apartment.

CAR ENGINE STOPS. CAR DOOR SHUTS. STEPS ON THE GRAVEL, SIGHING, PANTING AS PAUL'S CLIMBING UP THE BUILDING.

Paul: (INNER VOICE, OVER THE SOUND EFFECTS) Things were beginning to make more sense. But who would believe me? The police thought it was a joke. I needed evidence. And Maureen's help.

WINDOW GLASS SMASHED. SILENCE FOR 5 SECONDS. GUN LOADED. JUMPS INSIDE.

Paul: (YELLS) Don't move!
Rolf: (SURPRISED) What . . . what are you . . .
Paul: (VICTORIOUSLY) Sorry, Rolf. The game's over!

POLICE SIRENS IN THE DISTANCE.

APPENDIX C: ASSESSMENT OF AN ESSAY TASK

Write an essay about what grade you deserve for your participation in the Radio Drama Project. For the chance to receive the grade, you need to provide sufficient evidence with concrete examples. Address as many of the following points as possible:

- your own contribution to the group's product
- how you encouraged other group members to participate
- language skills you have mastered and/or practised
- other skills you have learnt
- language skills you will need to continue working on
- areas to focus on to improve your future group project works
- how you will be able to use what you have learnt when the course is over

CHAPTER 18

Ongoing Needs Analysis: English for Aviation in Brazil

Eliane H. Augusto-Navarro, Denise M. de Abreu-e-Lima,
and Luciana C. de Oliveira

Needs analysis is widely recognized as an essential instrument in English for specific purposes (ESP) because it guides course design by indicating what is specific about the language targeted in each particular case or context (Braine, 2001; Johns & Dudley-Evans, 1991; Johns & Price-Machado, 2001; Robinson, 1991). In Brazil, ESP became popular in the 1980s as a result of a proposition by the Catholic University of São Paulo to the Brazilian Education Council for a national ESP project (Holmes & Celani, 2006). Federal universities in the country became involved in this project aimed at teacher training, teaching material design and creating a resource and research center in ESP. As a consequence, ESP is still nationally interpreted as a synonym for a reading course because it was the only skill developed in the project. Although this national research center has been sustained for 25 years and has undergone evolution and reflection (Holmes & Celani, 2006), needs analysis does not seem to have received central attention. Most national ESP practice takes for granted that an initial interview or questionnaire is enough.

This chapter describes the steps taken to make the needs assessment process more ongoing, effective, and influential in program development for an ESP project for an aviation company in Brazil. It summarizes the main findings and results of this experience, highlighting the on-site target situation assessment and other ongoing needs analysis instruments used. The benefits from this assessment, which were applied to adapting the English for Aviation Program (EAVP), are discussed. The chapter shows that needs analyses should be done more than once to make such programs more effective.

CONTEXT

For 5 years, the Federal University of São Carlos, in the state of São Paulo, has offered English for Aviation (EAV) to the branch of a major Brazilian aviation company that takes care of aircraft checkup and maintenance. The EAVP started as a result of the company's wish to gain international certification in its job development. The company has some 1,000 employees who needed tailor-made courses in order to read maintenance manuals written in English. These adult language learners have English proficiency levels that are largely those of beginners. Most have a high school diploma but did not go to college. Each group of employees is responsible for a specific section of the aircraft, such as the hydraulic system, engine, landing gears, or upholstery.

Classes are taught four times a week within the company, and each group consists of 15–25 students organized by their proficiency levels. These students come from different sectors within the company and have diverse jobs. The team responsible for the program development consists of two English as a foreign language (EFL) university professors coordinating the activities; one graduate student working as a teaching assistant, helping the coordinators with the supervision and support of teachers; and five preservice EFL teachers who teach the classes. These preservice teachers were chosen by their academic records as well as by their previous teaching experience. Weekly meetings are held between a company representative and the course supervisor.

The courses are offered simultaneously with the employees' professional practice. Because these learners have very low levels of language proficiency and many have not had any formal studies for a number of years, we had to start with a course focus on general reading. But although their job requirements include the ability to read aircraft maintenance manuals written in English, initially most of the employees believed that the only way to learn a foreign language was by developing oral skills.

CURRICULUM, TASKS, MATERIALS

Four different types of needs analysis have been utilized throughout the EAVP teaching process. The first two involved interviews and questionnaires conducted with company management and employees. The third consisted of EFL teachers' written class reports. The fourth was an on-site target situation analysis (Dudley-Evans & St. John, 1998) with the team of teachers, workers, and their supervisors.

A present situation analysis (Dudley-Evans & St. John, 1998) was performed to determine the main issues by evaluating what learners could do linguistically in relation to what the company expected them to do in terms of EFL performance. This analysis consisted of a written test based on reading comprehension passages from aircraft maintenance manuals and a multiple-choice test of basic reading concepts. Because there is both turnover among the employees and an expansion of this branch of the company, this evaluation has been repeated many times.

Even when the company received its international certification, the aviation workers still struggled with the manuals. This was clearly detected through the third needs assessment instrument, the reports written by each teacher at the end of every class to evaluate course effectiveness in responding to the students' needs. Also, some learners said that they wanted to learn speaking and other skills in the class.

Johns and Dudley-Evans (1991) state that when an ESP course takes place along with students' professional requirements in the use of the language, their needs should be more apparent. But our practice has shown that this characteristic does not prevent students from revealing (mis)beliefs about how languages are learned and what is meant by learning a foreign language, even in an in-service English for occupational purposes context. These (mis)beliefs have a direct influence on students' wants, which do not always coincide with the sponsor's needs. In addition to pointing out that needs and wants are not necessarily integrated, an ESP curriculum should

> seek with the students the best way to satisfy all the parties involved . . . and . . . the apparent problem of a mis-match between learners' wants and the sponsor's need should be confronted and seen as the beginning of considerations and negotiation. (Hutchinson & Waters, 1984, p. 108)

Based on the need to consider students' wants, we changed the course design with the purpose of fulfilling students' expectations and, consequently, raising their motivation. By doing so, we shifted the focus from the company to the learners. As a result, there was too much emphasis on wants instead of needs, which made sponsors question the methodology used. The company management stated that the course emphasized listening and speaking, whereas the company's priority was technical reading.

As an illustration, some of the texts had been based on comics and song lyrics because the learners enjoyed them. These were replaced by texts from the aircraft maintenance manuals or by others about aviation. Constantly reminding the students about and discussing the purposes of the course (awareness raising) actually increased students' motivation for learning.

To take students' motivation and their real needs into consideration when designing materials, the coordinators decided to carry out another needs analysis. Because one of the main problems in designing the course had been that management cannot always clearly express company and employee needs, an on-site target situation assessment was used. This consisted of asking teachers to spend some time walking through different sectors at the company. These teachers were responsible for carefully watching the work routine, job shadowing, and taking detailed notes of every situation in which employees had to use English.

For 3 months, the teachers spent about 3 hours a week in either the hangar or the garages. They asked employees (their students in the EAV course) what they were doing and to what extent English was important for accomplishing their work. Soon after that, the teachers took notes on what they had observed in the learners' work routine that required their use of English. In these notes, they also contrasted what had been said with what they had noticed through observation, highlighting information that was not evident when they were in the classroom. In these on-site observation sessions, the teachers also interviewed the learners' supervisors about the EFL needs that they recognized for employees in their sectors. This fourth needs analysis was crucial in revealing details that influenced students' behavior in class, providing the coordinators with a more comprehensive view of the role of English in the company and, consequently, giving them more appropriate information to share and discuss with management. A summary of the needs analysis instruments, goals, and procedures is provided in the Appendix.

As a result of the various steps in this needs assessment process, there were two main kinds of administrative changes. The first was the hiring of an EFL graduate student with considerable experience in the EFL field to serve as a teaching assistant. She became responsible for observing classes, supporting teachers and learners, and keeping the company management informed about the course development, especially employees' attendance and performance. She filled an important gap between the company and the university. The second administrative change consisted of the company's designation of a management employee to support the course development. This person was responsible for identifying which employees had more urgent needs to improve their English skills and scheduling them to perform the present situation analysis tests. Both changes helped make the EAVP more productive.

In addition, four major pedagogical changes were identified and implemented in the program: students' awareness raising, materials development, course organization, and shared knowledge. In terms of awareness raising, it took time and planning to make students understand both why they were required to take an EAV course and some of the educational principles behind ESP. Nevertheless, as they learned that there was a strong team behind the course, their cooperation improved and so did their appreciation of the opportunity to take the course. As for the teaching materials, once the company's needs were reconsidered, more appropriate activities were developed.

At the same time, a variety of texts were offered besides aircraft maintenance manuals. Activities were developed based on what Hutchinson and Waters (1984) have called *parallel materials*. These consisted of texts about the history of aviation and security procedures inside aircrafts, scenes from movies involving aviation or aircraft as their theme, and extracts from airline magazines that can only be electronically accessed by employees. Moreover, written activities preparing students to write maintenance reports on repairs they had made on different parts of the aircraft were also included. These changes improved students' attendance and participation, and, in turn, teacher motivation, and ultimately the company's satisfaction with the course.

After the fourth needs analysis (on site), texts extracted from aircraft manuals were used in the design of teaching units. In addition, students started making reference to machines and other items in class that their teachers had seen during their visits. Before, on many occasions, teachers had never seen much of this equipment in the aircraft maintenance manuals. After the on-site analysis, students called teachers' attention to the fact that a given text referred to a certain piece of equipment, saying things such as "This is the machine you saw at my work section last week." The shared knowledge among the teachers and students made both parties feel more confident and comfortable in the classroom.

REFLECTIONS

This experience shows the importance of continuous and varied needs assessment instruments throughout the development of an ESP program. Several issues were noticed based on this experience. First, the teachers played an important role as researchers, reviewing their own practice and adapting the materials they had developed to reach new goals. Second, this experience has reassured the coordinators about the importance and role of needs analysis in ESP courses. And finally, it is desirable that ESP practitioners, as well as English language teaching professionals in general, become more aware that needs analysis must be used not only to specify linguistic needs but also in the learning context, as proposed by Hutchinson and Waters (1984) and Dudley-Evans and St. John (1998). Moreover, once is not enough in needs assessment; this evaluation has to be procedural and ongoing, repeated and varied, throughout the whole teaching–learning process.

Although we are aware that the situation described in this chapter is unique because of our support from the aviation company, the employees, and the teachers, we feel that it can be an example for other programs to improve their own needs assessments. We propose that similar programs take into consideration a number of items when preparing or redesigning an ESP curriculum.

First, consider teamwork involving teachers, a company representative, and a teacher, such as the teaching assistant in this case, who observes classes and helps the teachers evaluate successes and look for points of improvement. All of these team members should reflect together on possible solutions and redefinitions of the ESP work. Second, the program should use a variety of ongoing needs analyses, especially an on-site needs assessment instrument so that a program and materials can be developed that are as close as possible to the learners' target situation. These should reflect an insider's view of the process. Teachers should also be involved in the research by engaging them in the entire process of designing needs assessment instruments, analyzing the results, developing teaching materials, reflecting on the results, and linking them to theoretical readings and discussion about ESP practices. A weekly meeting of the team generally enables this practice. Finally, one should make sure that the adult language learners are aware of the course purposes and the sponsor's needs. These learners should be involved in the process by emphasizing the importance of their cooperation and, whenever possible, working with parallel materials that are of interest to them. To have a balance between needs and wants, the teaching team collects students' feedback about the course, the materials used, and teaching efficacy at the end of each course.

The experience outlined in this chapter reveals that teamwork and a constant reexamination of practice through analysis of the whole learning context makes a great difference in the development of a successful program. The positive outcomes are a direct result of the combined efforts of the university team with the full support of the company. When the parties involved are in close contact, both become more aware of each other's roles in teaching language for specific purposes.

Eliane H. Augusto-Navarro has a PhD in linguistics from São Paulo State University and has taught English for 21 years. She is the coordinator of the Graduate Program in Linguistics and a professor in EFL Teacher Education at Federal University of São Carlos, in Brazil. She has also co-coordinated the university's English for Aviation Program since 2003.

Denise M. de Abreu-e-Lima has a PhD in applied linguistics from the University of Campinas and has taught EFL for 25 years. She is the coordinator of the Open Distance Education Program at Federal University of São Carlos, in Brazil. She has also co-coordinated the English for Aviation Program since 2003. She is doing her postdoctoral research on distance education at Purdue University.

Luciana C. de Oliveira has a PhD in education from the University of California, Davis. She is assistant professor of literacy and language education at Purdue University, in Indiana, in the United States. She has been a consultant with the Federal University of São Carlos for 13 years and has more than 15 years of experience teaching English language learners at various levels.

APPENDIX: SUMMARY OF NEEDS ANALYSIS INSTRUMENTS, GOALS, AND PROCEDURES

Needs Analysis	Instrument	Goals	Procedures
Company management and staff	Interview	To determine company needs	At the beginning of each term, coordinators and management staff meet to determine the goals to be reached.
Employees (present situation analysis)	Written test, questionnaire	To evaluate employees' foreign language knowledge and language learning experience	At the beginning of each term, employees take tests to compare their improvement and opinions about their learning process.
Teachers' reports	Class reports	To evaluate the course effectiveness in responding to students' needs	At the end of each class, teachers write class reports.
On-site target situation analysis	On-site observation	To determine workers' real needs for using the target language	Teachers monitor different sectors at the company, observing work routine, job shadowing, and taking detailed notes of workers' use of English.

References

Annenberg Media. (1997–2009). *Session 1: Reader response. Theory overview.* Retrieved January 24, 2009, from http://www.learner.org/channel/workshops/hslit/session1/index.html

Appleton, J. (2004). "Jungle fever": Visualization and the implication for writing extensive readers. *Developing Teachers.com.* Retrieved January 24, 2009, from http://www.developingteachers.com/articles_tchtraining/junglefever1_jo.htm

Audacity (Version 1.2.6) [Computer software]. (2006). Audacity Development Team. http://audacity.sourceforge.net/

Auerbach, E. (1992). *Making meaning making change: Participatory curriculum development for adult ESL literacy.* McHenry, IL: Delta Systems.

Australian Universities Teaching Committee. (2002). *Minimising plagiarism.* University of Melbourne. Retrieved September 10, 2008, from http://www.cshe.unimelb.edu.au/assessinglearning/03/plagMain.html

Avruch, K. (2002). What do I need to know about culture? A researcher says . . . In J. Lederach & J. Jenner (Eds.), *A handbook of international peacebuilding: Into the eye of the storm* (pp. 75–87). San Francisco: Jossey-Bass.

Bamford, J., & Day, R. R. (2004). *Extensive reading activities for teaching language.* New York: Cambridge University Press.

Basturkmen, H. (2002). Negotiating meaning in seminar-type discussion and EAP. *English for Specific Purposes, 21,* 233–242.

Belbin, R. M. (1993). *Team roles at work.* Oxford: Butterworth-Heinemann.

Benson, P. (2007). Autonomy in language teaching and learning. *Language Teaching, 40,* 21–40.

Bhatia, V. K. (2004). *Worlds of written discourse: A genre-based view.* London: Continuum.

Biggs, J. B. (1996). Western misperceptions of the Confucian-heritage learning culture. In D. A. Watkins & J. B. Biggs (Eds.), *The Chinese learner: Cultural, psychological and contextual influences* (pp. 46–67). Hong Kong: Comparative Education Research Centre.

Blackboard. (1997–2009). *Blackboard*. Retrieved February 19, 2009, from http://www.blackboard.com/

Borras, I., & Lafayette, R. (1994). Effects of multimedia courseware subtitling on the speaking performance of college students of French. *Modern Language Journal, 78,* 61–75.

Braine, G. (2001). Twenty years of needs analyses: Reflections on a personal journey. In J. Flowerdew & M. Peacock (Eds.), *Research perspectives on English for academic purposes* (pp. 195–207). New York: Cambridge University Press.

Brandt, C. (2006). *Success on your certificate course in English language teaching: A guide to becoming a teacher in ELT/TESOL.* London: Sage.

Brandt, C. (2007). Allowing for learning: A critical issue for TESOL certificate course tutors. *English Language Teacher Education and Development, 10,* 1–9.

Brinton, D., & Master, P. (Eds.). (1997). *New ways in content-based instruction.* Alexandria, VA: TESOL.

Bruner, J. (1996). *The culture of education.* Cambridge, MA: Harvard University Press.

Buchanan, H. (1992). *ESL field trips: Maximizing the experience both in and out of the classroom.* Unpublished master's thesis, School for International Training, Brattleboro, VT. (ERIC Document Reproduction Service No. ED352838)

Campbell, G. (2005). There's something in the air: Podcasting in education. *Educause Review, 40*(6), 33–46.

Category:Controversies. (2008). Retrieved January 24, 2009, from http://en.wikipedia.org/wiki/Category:Controversies

CELTA syllabus. (n.d.). Retrieved January 22, 2009, from http://www.cambridgeesol.org/assets/pdf/celta8_251103.pdf

Certificate in English Language Teaching to Adults (CELTA). (n.d.). Retrieved April 9, 2009, from http://www.cambridgeesol.org/exams/teaching-awards/celta.html

Clankie, S. M. (2000). Teaching students to evaluate Internet source material. *TESOL Journal, 9*(2), 33–34.

Clark, J. (2001). Stimulating collaboration and discussion in online learning environments. *The Internet and Higher Education, 4,* 119–124.

Cohen, A. D. (1998). *Strategies in learning and using a second language.* London: Longman.

Cohen, A. D., & Oxford, R. (2003). The learner's side of foreign language learning: Where do styles, strategies, and tasks meet? *International Review of Applied Linguistics in Language Teaching, 41,* 279–291.

Cole, M. (1991). Conclusion. In L. B. Resnick, J. M. Levin, & S. Teasley (Eds.), *Perspectives on socially shared cognition* (pp. 398–417). Washington, DC: American Psychological Association.

Collins, M. L. (1978). Effects of enthusiasm training on preservice elementary teachers. *Research in Teacher Education, 16*(1), 53–57.

Controversial podcasts. (n.d.). Retrieved January 24, 2009, from http://web.mac .com/joseph_dias/iWeb/controversy/Podcast/Archive.html

Cook, G. (1994). Repetition and learning by heart: An aspect of intimate discourse, and its implications. *ELT Journal, 48,* 133–139.

Cook, V. (2001). Using the first language in the classroom. *Canadian Modern Language Review, 57,* 402–423.

Cook, V. (Ed.). (2002). *Portraits of the L2 user.* Clevedon, England: Multilingual Matters.

Corder, S. (1967). The significance of learners' errors. *International Review of Applied Linguistics, 5*(4), 161–169.

Costello, M. L., Brunner, P. W., & Hasty, K. (2002). Preparing students for the empowered workplace. *Active Learning in Higher Education, 3,* 117–127.

Csikszentmihalyi, M. (1997). Intrinsic motivation and effective teaching: A flow analysis. In J. L. Bess (Ed.), *Teaching well and liking it* (pp. 73–89). London: Johns Hopkins University Press.

Daudelin, M. W. (1996). Learning from experience through reflection. *Organizational Dynamics, 24*(3), 36–48.

Davis, B. (1993). *Tools for teaching.* San Francisco: Jossey-Bass.

Dawson, N. (2005). *Penguin Readers teacher's guide to using graded readers.* London: Pearson Education. Retrieved January 24, 2009, from http://www.penguinreaders .com/downloads/PRTGUsingGradedReaders.pdf

Day, R. R., & Bamford, J. (1998). *Extensive reading in the second language classroom.* New York: Cambridge University Press.

Deoksoon's podcast. (n.d.). Retrieved January 22, 2009, from http://deoksoon .podomatic.com/

Diaz, D., Justicia, N., & Levine, L. (2002). *Making content accessible to promote second language acquisition: The ESL intensive program at Hostos Community College (CUNY).* Bronx, NY: Hostos Community College. (ERIC Document Reproduction Service No. ED477556)

Ding, P. (2008). *The nature and impact of teacher enthusiasm in second language learning.* Unpublished doctoral dissertation, University of Nottingham, Nottingham, England.

Dodge, B. (2007). *Webquest.org.* Retrieved January 28, 2009, from http://webquest .org/

Dörnyei, Z. (2006). Individual differences in second language acquisition. *AILA Review, 19*(1), 42–68.

Dörnyei, Z., & Murphey, T. (2003). *Group dynamics in the language classroom.* Cambridge: Cambridge University Press.

Doughty, C., & Williams, J. (1998). Pedagogical choices in focus on form. In C. Doughty & J. Williams (Eds.), *Focus on form in classroom second language acquisition* (pp. 197–261). Cambridge: Cambridge University Press.

Dudley-Evans, T., & St. John, M. J. (1998). *Developments in English for specific purposes: A multidisciplinary approach.* New York: Cambridge University Press.

El-Shamy, S. (2005). *Role play made easy: 25 structured rehearsals for managing problem situations and dealing with difficult people.* San Francisco: Pfeiffer.

Ellis, N., & Larsen-Freeman, D. (2006). Language emergence: Implications for applied linguistics. *Applied Linguistics, 27,* 558–589.

Ellis, R. (2005a). *Instructed second language acquisition: A literature review.* Wellington, New Zealand: Ministry of Education. Retrieved January 26, 2009, from http://www.educationcounts.govt.nz/__data/assets/pdf_file/0008/6983/ instructed-second-language.pdf

Ellis, R. (2005b). Principles of instructed language learning. *Asian EFL Journal, 7*(3), 9–24.

Ericksen, S. C. (1984). *The essence of good teaching.* San Francisco: Jossey-Bass.

Fasheh, M. (2003). *The "World Social Forum" in Porto Alegre, Brazil: Manifestation of a new phase in human history.* Retrieved January 26, 2009, from http://www .almoultaqa.com/ar22.aspx

Ferdman, B. (1990). Literacy and cultural identity. *Harvard Educational Review, 60,* 181–205.

Ferguson, G., & Donno, S. (2003). One-month teacher training courses: Time for a change? *ELT Journal, 57,* 26–33.

Flowerdew, L. (1998). A cultural perspective on group work. *ELT Journal, 52,* 323–329.

Freire, P. (1983). *Pedagogy of the oppressed.* New York: Continuum.

Fries, C., & Fries, A. (1961). *Foundations of English.* Tokyo: Kenkyusha.

Furr, M. (2007). Reading circles: Moving great stories from the periphery of the language classroom to its center. *Language Teacher, 31*(5), 15–18.

GarageBand (Version 5.0.1) [Computer software]. (2009). Cupertino, CA: Apple. http://www.apple.com/ilife/garageband/

Gardner, D., & Miller, L. (1999). *Establishing self-access: From theory to practice.* Cambridge: Cambridge University Press.

Gee, J. (1989). Literacy, discourse, and linguistics: Introduction. *Journal of Education, 171*(1), 5–17.

Ghahremani-Ghajar, S., Mirhosseini, S. A., & Fattahi, H. (2007, July). *Living the language of pain: A language-discovery approach to medical English.* Paper presented at the Fourth Conference on Issues in English Language Teaching in Iran, Tehran.

Good, T. L., & Brophy, J. E. (2000). *Looking in classrooms.* Boston: Pearson Education.

Google. (1999–2009). *Blogger.* Retrieved January 24, 2009, from https://www.blogger.com/

Google. (2009a). *Google groups.* Retrieved January 24, 2009, from http://groups.google.com/

Google. (2009b). *Google sites.* Retrieved January 22, 2009, from http://sites.google.com/

Graddol, D. (2006). *English next: Why global English may mean the end of English as a foreign language.* London: British Council.

Griffiths, C. (2008). Age and good language learners. In C. Griffiths (Ed.), *Lessons from good language learners* (pp. 35–48). Cambridge: Cambridge University Press.

Guceri, M., & Akin, A. R. (1998). Case studies in education. *Forum 36*(4), 18–24.

Hale, C. (2006). Challenging tradition: Establishing a self-access language learning centre in an East Asian academic high school (Japan). In T. Farrell (Ed.), *Language teacher research in Asia* (pp. 75–90). Alexandria, VA: TESOL.

Harmer, J. (2001). *The practice of English language teaching.* Harlow, England: Pearson.

Harris, R. (1995). Overseas students in the United Kingdom university system, *Higher Education, 29,* 77–92.

Hedge, T. (2000). *Teaching and learning in the language classroom.* Oxford: Oxford University Press.

Hills, H. (2001). *Team-based learning.* Hampshire, England: Gower.

Holec, H. (1981). *Autonomy and foreign language learning.* Oxford: Pergamon Press.

Holmes, J. L., & Celani, M. A. A. (2006). Sustainability and local knowledge: The case of the Brazilian ESP project 1980–2005. *English for Specific Purposes, 25,* 109–122.

Hutchinson, T., & Waters, A. (1984). How communicative is ESP? *ELT Journal, 38,* 108–113.

Hutchinson, T., & Waters, A. (1987). *English for specific purposes: A learning-centered approach.* Cambridge: Cambridge University Press.

Hymes, D. (1972). On communicative competence. In J. Pride & J. Holmes (Eds.), *Sociolinguistics* (pp. 269–293). Harmondsworth, England: Penguin.

Jackson, J. (2002). The China strategy: A tale of two case leaders. *English for Specific Purposes, 21,* 243–259.

Jenkins, J. (2006). Current perspectives on teaching world Englishes and English as a lingua franca. *TESOL Quarterly, 40,* 157–181.

Johns, A. M., & Dudley-Evans, T. (1991). English for specific purposes: International in scope, specific in purpose. *TESOL Quarterly, 25,* 297–314.

Johns, A. M., & Price-Machado, D. (2001). English for specific purposes: Tailoring courses to student needs—and to the outside world. In M. Celce-Murcia (Ed.), *Teaching English as a second or foreign language* (3rd ed., pp. 43–54). Boston: Heinle & Heinle.

Johnson, D. W., & Johnson, R. T. (1995). *Creative controversy: Intellectual challenge in the classroom* (3rd ed.). Edina, MN: Interaction Book Company.

Johnson, D., Johnson, R., & Holubec, E. (1993). *Circles of learning* (4th ed.). Edina, MN: Interaction Book Company.

Johnson, D. W., Johnson, R. T., & Stanne, M. B. (2000). *Cooperative learning methods: A meta-analysis.* Retrieved January 24, 2009, from http://www.co-operation.org/pages/cl-methods.html

Katzenbach, J. R., & Smith, D. K. (1993). The discipline of teams. *Harvard Business Review, 71*(2), 115.

Keily, R. (2004). Learning to critique in EAP. *Journal of English for Academic Purposes, 3,* 211–227.

Kim, D. (2009). Innovative educational technology in the global classroom. *Essential Teacher, 6*(1), 37–39.

Knowles, M. S., Holton, E. F., & Swanson, R. A. (1998). *The adult learner: The definitive classic in adult education and human resource development* (5th ed.). Houston, TX: Gulf.

Krashen, S. (1982). *Principles and practice in second language acquisition.* Oxford: Pergamon Press.

Krashen, S. (1993). *The power of reading.* Englewood, CO: Libraries Unlimited.

Kubanyiova, M. (2004). Leave them alone. *English Teaching Professional, 33,* 13–14.

Lado, R. (1957). *Linguistics across cultures.* Ann Arbor: University of Michigan Press.

Ladousse, G. (1987). *Role play.* Oxford: Oxford University Press.

LAME (Version 3.98.1) [Computer software]. (2008). http://lame.sourceforge.net/

Lantolf, J. (Ed). (2000). *Sociocultural theory and second language learning.* Oxford: Oxford University Press.

Laurillard, D. (2002). *Rethinking university teaching: A framework for the effective use of learning technologies.* London: RoutledgeFalmer.

Lave, J., & Wenger, E. (1991). *Situated learning: Legitimate peripheral participation.* Cambridge: Cambridge University Press.

Lewicki, R., Saunders, D., & Minton, J. (2001). Negotiation: Framing, strategizing, and planning. In R. Lewicki, B. Barry, & D. Saunders (Eds.), *Essentials of negotiation* (2nd ed., pp. 22–53). New York: McGraw-Hill.

Lick, D. W. (2006). A new perspective on organizational learning: Creating learning teams. *Evaluation and Program Planning, 29,* 88–96.

Light, R. (2001). *Making the most of college: Students speak their minds.* Cambridge, MA: Harvard University Press.

Lightbown, P. (1992). Can they do it themselves? A comprehension-based ESL course for young children. In R. Courchêne, J. St. John, C. Therrien, & J. Glidden (Eds.), *Comprehension-based language teaching: Current trends* (pp. 353–370). Ottawa, Ontario, Canada: Ottawa University Press.

Little, D., Ridley, J., & Ushioda, E. (2003). *Learner autonomy in the foreign language classroom: Teacher, learner, curriculum and assessment.* Dublin, Ireland: Authentik.

Long, M. (1996). The role of the linguistic environment in second language acquisition. In W. Ritchie & T. Bhatia (Eds.), *Handbook of second language acquisition* (pp. 413–468). San Diego, CA: Academic Press.

Long, M., & Crookes, G. (1992). Three approaches to task-based language teaching. *TESOL Quarterly, 26,* 27–56.

Lyster, R. (1998). Recasts, repetition and ambiguity in L2 classroom discourse. *Studies in Second Language Acquisition, 20,* 51–80.

Lyster, R. (2007). *Learning and teaching languages through content: A counterbalanced approach.* Amsterdam: John Benjamins.

Mackey, W. F. (1991). Language education in bilingual Acadia: An experiment in redressing the balance. In O. Garcia (Ed.), *Bilingual education* (pp. 239–249). Amsterdam: John Benjamins.

Mageean, B., & Hai, C. (1999). *New thinking on automaticity and memorisation.* Retrieved January 23, 2009, from http://www.aare.edu.au/98pap/mag98091.htm

Mantovani, G. (1996). *New communication environments: From everyday to virtual.* London: Taylor & Francis.

McCurdy, D., Spradley, J., & Shandy, D. (2005). *The cultural experience: Ethnography in a complex society* (2nd ed.). Long Grove, IL: Waveland Press.

Miller, G. (Producer/Director/Writer). (1992). *Lorenzo's Oil* [Motion picture]. United States: Universal Pictures.

Mirhosseini, S. A. (2007). Real flowers or plastic flowers in learning medical English. *Asian ESP Journal, 3*(1), 108–112.

Mohan, B. (1986). *Language and content.* Reading, MA: Addison-Wesley.

Murphy, J. M., & Stoller, F. L. (2001). Sustained-content language teaching: An emerging definition. *TESOL Journal, 10*(2–3), 3–5.

Murphy, L. (2007). Supporting learner autonomy: Theory and practice in a distance learning context. In D. Gardner (Ed.), *Learner autonomy 10: Integration and support* (pp. 72–92). Dublin, Ireland: Authentik.

Murray, G., & Bollinger, D. (2001). Developing cross-cultural awareness: Learning through the experiences of others. *TESL Canada Journal, 19*(1), 62–72.

Ning. (2008). Retrieved January 22, 2009, from http://www.ning.com/

Norton, B., & Toohey, K. (2001). Changing perspectives on good language learners. *TESOL Quarterly, 35,* 307–322.

Norton, B., & Toohey, K. (Eds.). (2004). *Critical pedagogies and language learning.* Cambridge: Cambridge University Press.

Oanh, D. T. H., & Hien, N. T. (2006). Memorization and EFL students' strategies at university level in Vietnam. *TESL-EJ, 10*(2). Retrieved January 23, 2009, from http://tesl-ej.org/ej38/a4.pdf

Ohta, A. (1995). Applying sociocultural theory to an analysis of learner discourse: Learner-learner collaborative interaction in the zone of proximal development. *Issues in Applied Linguistics, 6*(2), 93–121.

O'Malley, J. M., & Chamot, A. U. (1990). *Learning strategies in second language acquisition.* Cambridge: Cambridge University Press.

Oxford, R. L. (2003). Toward a more systematic model of L2 learner autonomy. In D. Palfreyman & R. C. Smith (Eds.), *Learner autonomy across cultures* (pp. 75–91). Basingstoke, England: Palgrave Macmillan.

PacDV free sound effects. (n.d.). Retrieved January 26, 2009, from http://www.pacdv.com/sounds/index.html

Palermo, A. E. (1996–2006). *Tony Palermo's RuyaSonic site*. Retrieved January 26, 2009, from http://ruyasonic.com/

Peace Corps. (2003). *An NGO training guide for Peace Corps volunteers*. Retrieved January 24, 2009, from http://www.peacecorps.gov/multimedia/pdf/library/M0070_intro.pdf

Pennycook, A. (1999). Introduction: Critical approaches to TESOL. *TESOL Quarterly, 33*, 329–348.

Peters, O. (1998). *Learning and teaching in distance education: Analyses and interpretations from an international perspective*. London: Kogan Page.

Pizzorno, M. (2006). Welcome to my Web: Preparing second language students for college and university academic settings through information literacy and the Internet. In M. A. Snow & L. Kamhi-Stein (Eds.), *Developing a new course for adult learners* (pp. 261–284). Alexandria, VA: TESOL.

PodOmatic. (2009). Retrieved January 22, 2009, from http://www.podomatic.com/

Ponder, R., & Powell, B. (2001). Sourcebooks in a sustained-content curriculum. *TESOL Journal, 10*(2),18–22.

Radio Willow Web. (n.d.). Retrieved January 22, 2009, from http://www.mpsomaha.org/willow/radio/listen.html

Ramburuth, P. (2001, May). Cross cultural learning behaviour in higher education: Perceptions versus practice. *UltiBASE*. Retrieved January 23, 2009, from http://ultibase.rmit.edu.au/Articles/may01/ramburuth1.htm

Richards, J. (Ed.). (1998). *Teaching in action: Case studies from second language classrooms*. Alexandria, VA: TESOL.

Richards, J. C. (2001). Postscript: The ideology of TESOL. In R. Carter & D. Nunan (Eds.), *The Cambridge guide to teaching English to speakers of other languages* (pp. 213–217). Cambridge: Cambridge University Press.

Richardson, W. (2006). Making waves [Electronic version]. *School Library Journal, 52*(10), 54–56.

Roberts, C., Byram, M., Barro, A., Jordan, S., & Street, B. (2001). *Language learners as ethnographers*. Clevedon, England: Multilingual Matters.

Robinson, P. (1991). *ESP today: A practitioner's guide*. Hemel Hempstead, England: Prentice Hall International.

Robinson, P. (2005). Aptitude and second language acquisition. *Annual Review of Applied Linguistics, 25*, 46–73.

Robinson-Stuart, G., & Nocon, H. (1996). Second culture acquisition: Ethnography in the foreign language classroom. *Modern Language Journal, 80*, 431–449.

Rodgers, T. S. (2001). Language teaching methodology. Retrieved January 26, 2009, from http://www.cal.org/resources/digest/rodgers.html

Salmon, P. (1988). *Psychology for teachers: An alternative approach.* London: Hutchinson.

Samovar, L., & Porter, R. E. (2000). Introduction. In L. Samovar & R. E. Porter (Eds.), *Intercultural communication: A reader* (9th ed.; pp. 5–16). Belmont, CA: Wadsworth.

Samuelowicz, K. (1987). Learning problems of overseas students: Two sides of a story. *Higher Education Research and Development, 6,* 121–133.

Schmidt, R. (1990). The role of consciousness in second language learning. *Applied Linguistics, 11,* 17–46.

Schumann, J. (1986). Research on the acculturation model for second language acquisition. *Journal of Multilingual and Multicultural Development, 7,* 379–392.

Segalowitz, N. (2000). Automaticity and attentional skill in fluent performance. In H. Rigenbach (Ed.), *Perspectives on fluency* (pp. 200–219). Ann Arbor: University of Michigan Press.

Selinker, L. (1972). Interlanguage. *International Review of Applied Linguistics, 10,* 209–231.

Senior, R. (2002). A class-centred approach to language teaching. *ELT Journal, 56,* 397–403.

Sherman, G. (2006). Instructional roles of electronic portfolios. In A. Jafari & C. Kaufman (Eds.), *Handbook of research on e-portfolios* (pp. 1–19). London: Idea Group Reference.

Skehan, P. (1989). *Individual differences in second language learning.* London: Arnold.

Skehan, P. (1998). *A cognitive approach to language learning.* Oxford: Oxford University Press.

Somé, M. P. (1998). *The healing wisdom of Africa: Finding life purpose through nature, ritual, and community.* New York: Tarcher/Putnam.

Spradley, J. P. (1979). *The ethnographic interview.* New York: Holt Reinhart and Winston.

Sprankle, B. (n.d.). *Room 208.* Retrieved January 22, 2009, from http://www.bobsprankle.com/blog/

Squires, G. (1993). Education for adults. In M. Thorpe, R. Edwards, & A. Hanson (Eds.), *Culture and processes of adult learning* (pp. 87–108). London: Routledge.

Strevens, P. (1977). Special-purpose language learning: A perspective. *Language Teaching and Linguistics Abstracts, 10(3),* 145–163.

SurveyMonkey.com. (1999–2009). *SurveyMonkey*. Retrieved March 2, 2009, from http://www.surveymonkey.com/

Thiroux, E. (1999). *The critical edge: Thinking and researching in a virtual society*. Upper Saddle River, NJ: Prentice-Hall.

Thorpe, M. (2002). Rethinking learner support: The challenge of collaborative online learning. *Open Learning, 17*(2), 105–119.

Ting-Toomey, S., & Chung, L. C. (2005). *Understanding intercultural communication*. Los Angeles: Roxbury.

Trinity College London. (2006). *Certificate in teaching English to speakers of other languages (CertTESOL)*. Retrieved February 9, 2009, from http://www .trinitycollege.co.uk/resource/?id=1770

Tusting, K., & Barton, D. (2003). *Models of adult learning: A literature review*. Leicester, England: National Research and Development Centre for Adult Literacy and Numeracy.

University of South Florida. (2007). *USF on iTunes U*. Retrieved January 22, 2009, from http://itunes.usf.edu/

Vivisimo. (2004–2009). *Clusty*. Retrieved January 24, 2009, from http://clusty .com/

Vygotsky, L. S. (1978). *Mind in society: The development of higher psychological processes*. Cambridge, MA: Harvard University Press.

Walker, C. (2001). *Penguin Readers teacher's guide to using best sellers*. London: Penguin Longman. Retrieved January 24, 2009, from http://www.penguinreaders .com/downloads/prteachersguides/PRTGUsingBestsellers.pdf

Watson-Gegeo, K. (2004). Mind, language, and epistemology: Toward a language socialization paradigm for SLA. *Modern Language Journal, 88,* 331–350.

Wenden, A. (1998). Metacognitive knowledge and language learning. *Applied Linguistics, 19,* 515–537.

Wenger, E. (1999). *Communities of practice: Learning, meaning and identity*. Cambridge: Cambridge University Press.

White, R. V. (1988). *The ELT curriculum*. Oxford: Blackwell.

Widdowson, H. (1978). *Teaching language as communication*. Oxford: Oxford University Press.

Wilkins, D. (1976). *Notional syllabuses*. Oxford: Oxford University Press.

Williams, M., & Burden, R. L. (1997). *Psychology for language teachers: A social constructivist approach*. Cambridge: Cambridge University Press.

Windschitl, M. (2000). Constructing understanding. In P. B. Joseph, S. L. Bravmann, M. A. Windschitl, E. R. Mikel, & N. S. Green (Eds.), *Cultures of curriculum* (pp. 95–136). Mahwah, NJ: Lawrence Erlbaum.

Wiske, M. S. (1998). *Teaching for understanding: Linking research with practice.* San Francisco: Jossey-Bass.

Wissot, J. (1970). The English-as-a-second-language trip: Its structure and value. *TESOL Quarterly, 4,* 165–168.

WordPress. (n.d.). Retrieved January 24, 2009, from http://wordpress.org/

World Learning. (2009). *SIT Graduate Institute TESOL certificate.* Retrieved February 9, 2009, from http://www.sit.edu/graduate/5191.htm

Wurr, A. (2002). Language experience approach revisited: The use of personal narratives in adult L2 literacy instruction. *Reading Matrix, 2*(1). Retrieved January 23, 2009, from http://www.readingmatrix.com/articles/wurr/index.html

Yahoo! (2008). *Yahoo! groups.* Retrieved January 24, 2009, from http://groups .yahoo.com/

Yang, N.-D. (2003). Integrating portfolios into learning strategy-based instruction for EFL college students. *International Review of Applied Linguistics in Language Teaching, 41,* 293–317.

YouTube. (2008). *YouTube.* Retrieved January 24, 2009, from http://www.youtube .com

Index

Page numbers followed by an *f* or *t* indicate figures or tables.

Also Available From TESOL

TESOL Classroom Practice Series
M. Dantas-Whitney, S. Rilling, and L. Savova, Series Editors

Classroom Management
Thomas S. C. Farrell, Editor

Using Textbooks Effectively
Lilia Savova, Editor

Insights on Teaching Speaking in TESOL
Tim Stewart, Editor

Authenticity in the Classroom and Beyond: Adult Learners
Sarah Rilling and Maria Dantas-Whitney, Editors

Language Games: Innovative Activities for Teaching English
Maureen Snow Adrade, Editor

❀ ❀ ❀ ❀ ❀

Language Teacher Research Series
Thomas S. C. Farrell, Series Editor

Language Teacher Research in Africa
Leketi Makalela, Editor

Language Teacher Research in Asia
Thomas S. C. Farrell, Editor

Language Teacher Research in Europe
Simon Borg, Editor

Language Teacher Research in the Americas
Hedy McGarrell, Editor

Language Teacher Research in the Middle East
Christine Coombe and Lisa Barlow, Editors

Language Teacher Research in Australia and New Zealand
Jill Burton and Anne Burns, Editors

❀ ❀ ❀ ❀ ❀

Perspectives on Community College ESL Series
Craig Machado, Series Editor

Volume 1: Pedagogy, Programs, Curricula, and Assessment
Marilynn Spaventa, Editor

Volume 2: Students, Mission, and Advocacy
Amy Blumenthal, Editor

Volume 3: Faculty, Administration, and the Working Environment
Jose A.Carmona, Editor

✳ ✳ ✳ ✳ ✳

Collaborative Partnerships Between ESL and Classroom Teachers Series
Debra Suarez, Series Editor

Helping English Language Learners Succeed in Pre-K–12 Elementary Schools
Jan Lacina, Linda New Levine, and Patience Sowa

Helping English Language Learners Succeed in Middle and High Schools
Faridah Pawan and Ginger Sietman, Editors

✳ ✳ ✳ ✳ ✳

TESOL Language Curriculum Development Series
Kathleen Graves, Series Editor

Planning and Teaching Creatively Within a Required Curriculum for Adult Learners
Anne Burns and Helen de Silva Joyce, Editors

Revitalizing an Established Program for Adult Learners
Alison Rice, Editors

Developing a New Curriculum for Adult Learners
Michael Carroll, Editor

Developing a New Course for Adult Learners
Lía Kamhi-Stein and Marguerite Ann Snow

✳ ✳ ✳ ✳ ✳

CALL Environments: Research, Practice, and Critical Issues, 2nd ed.
Joy Egbert and Elizabeth Hanson-Smith, Editors

Learning Languages through Technology
Elizabeth Hanson-Smith and Sarah Rilling, Editors

Global English Teaching and Teacher Education: Praxis and Possibility
Seran Dogancay-Aktuna and Joel Hardman, Editors

Local phone: (240)646-7037
Fax: (301)206-9789
E-Mail: tesolpubs@brightkey.net
Toll-free: 1-888-891-0041
Mail Orders to TESOL, P.O. Box 79283, Baltimore, MD 21279-0283
ORDER ONLINE at www.tesol.org and click on "Bookstore"